**the Son of God
is dancing…**

To Peter,
God bless
[signature] o Bridget

"When the Son of God is dancing,
the devil can't come near …"

(Zambian children's chorus)

the Son of God is dancing...

A Message of Hope

Adrian and Bridget Plass

11 10 09 08 07 06 05   7 6 5 4 3 2 1

First published 2005 by Authentic Media,
9 Holdom Avenue, Bletchley, Milton Keynes, MK1 1QR, UK
and 129 Mobilization Drive, Waynesboro, GA 30830-4575, USA
www.authenticmedia.co.uk

British Library Cataloguing in Publication Data

A catalogue record for this book is available
from the British Library

ISBN 1-85078-607-0

All photography by Jim Loring, Bridget Plass and Peter Scott

Cover design by Sam Redwood
Typeset by GCS, Leighton Buzzard, Beds.
Print Management by Adare Carwin
Printed and Bound by J. H. Haynes & Co. Ltd., Sparkford

To Penelope,
the most important person in the world

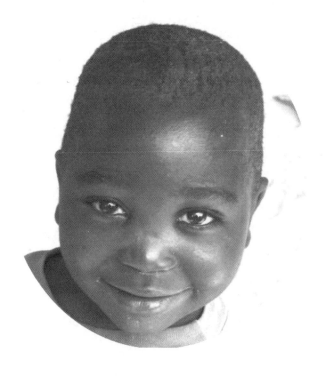

Contents

Acknowledgements

We would like to thank those in the UK World Vision office, and many, many individuals in Zambia itself who made this trip possible and profitable. Some of their names appear in this book, but many do not. Their hospitality, vulnerability and sheer hard work have been a real gift to us. We would also like to thank our daughter Kate for once again accepting our disappearance with good grace, and our sons for their warm support at the end of the phone.

Note: Each piece in this book is preceded by 'A' or 'B'. Quick-witted readers will not be surprised to learn that the 'A' sections are written by Adrian, and the 'B' ones by Bridget.

Introduction

B: I am sitting in my car, stuck in a typical Sussex traffic jam, and I am having an impassioned discussion – me with myself! Or rather me with the mental images of those who have made comments about HIV/AIDS in Africa since our return from Zambia.

Comments such as:

"Well, of course, we all know about African men. I mean, they can't be bothered – don't respect women enough – animal instincts, if you know what I mean."

"And then, of course, there's the government. I mean, why don't they sort it out?"

"I don't like to say it but, well you know, they've brought it on themselves."

"Mind you, there's always a problem with lethargy when it comes to Africa. They're still in the dark ages, aren't they? The women just put up with everything. They don't seem able to say no."

I have to remind myself, as I find myself beginning to boil inside, that these apparently civilized folk who are so ready with their comments are, in fact, underprivileged and, because of their circumstances, the poorest of the poor.

"So," I graciously conclude as eventually my car crawls forward, "I suppose I have to excuse this ignorance, since none of you have actually had the opportunity we did to see for ourselves what is actually happening."

It was to the dry and dusty village of Zamtan that we travelled with Peter Scott, our old friend from World Vision, and Jim Loring, a professional photographer, to witness not only the devastation wrought by the disease, but also the strides taken by an extraordinary group of individuals who are surviving the pandemic and working to curb its effects.

Individuals like Rodrick, shopkeeper and chairman of the Zamtan Committee, which has the overall responsibility for running the project, including the care of orphans and vulnerable children. Solemn, funny, passionate, loyal, committed, this man is working flat out for those in his immediate community whose needs he sees as greater than his own. Then there is Femmy Knola. The 56 dying women she personally cares for call her 'Mother'. Thom Kasuba, development facilitator for HIV/AIDS initiatives, whose calm exterior houses a heart burning for the poorest of the poor. Phyllis Chintu heads up the Home Care Team with an enthusiasm and thoroughness that would never allow any intrepid microbes or superbugs to darken the doorstep of any ward of which she was in charge (if we were ever lucky enough to have her in one of our hospitals). We met Lackson and Philemon, orphans and rat catchers par excellence. David and Elizabeth Daka care for nine orphans. And then there is Fordson himself, the eloquent, educated and energetic project manager.

We visited the border between Zambia and the Congo, where we met truckers and prostitutes and those who work with them at the Corridors of Hope centres – people like Berry and Eunice, teenage prostitutes and mothers who, with help, are turning their lives around. Beautiful Chilufya, whose story moved us to tears. And the diminutive Auntie Doris, all five-feet-one-inch of her, challenging burly truck drivers to use condoms.

Few people will ever have the privilege of encountering these unforgettable characters in person, but you will meet them in the pages of this book. Each one contributes his or her own steps, style and colour to the dance that is beginning to lead their communities away from death and towards new life.

1. Unplugged in Zamtan

A: I mistrust any device or appliance that describes itself as having 'universal' application. The claim is never justified. Whether the 'universal' roof-rack that we once bought might have fitted every other type of car in the universe is impossible to know. All I can tell you for sure is that it did not fit ours.

Electrical plug adaptors that are 'suitable for use in all countries of the world' have the same drawback. They have always dumbly refused to adapt to the sockets of the specific country that we happen to be visiting. This time we were determined to crack it. Given an available power supply at our accommodation in Zambia, we were jolly well going to have the use of such items as hairdryers, phone chargers and the rest of our little clutch of electrical aids to comfortable living.

At Heathrow Airport we found a shop specializing in travel accessories, including plug adaptors. Being the old hands that it has taken us two decades to finally become, we ignored the one that would have functioned in every single corner of the solar system other than Southern Africa and plumped for a set of nine or ten different plug fascias, all in a little satin bag with a drawstring. Neat. Nice.

Twenty-four hours later, sitting in our Lusaka hotel room as we waited for our crumpled bodies to resume their normal shape after the long flight, we were able to test our purchase. And it worked! One of the adaptors adapted. Appliances applied themselves. They buzzed and clicked and charged just as they normally did at home. What a relief. We were plugged in.

Two days later, perched on a rickety chair outside a shabby dwelling in the community of Zamtan, struggling not to reveal my horror at seeing the condition of a victim of the AIDS pandemic, I remembered that little set of adaptors and felt myself going cold inside.

We met the lady in question on our first full day in dusty Zamtan, one of three neighbouring communities in which World Vision has supported an Area Development Programme (ADP) for the last three years. Zambia is one of the least wealthy countries in the world, and residents of the areas we were visiting are among the poorest of the poor. There is no litter in a place like Zamtan. That is because there is no excess, no packaged goods, no discarded scraps of food. You never discard food. You eat it. Many are living below starvation level, and the creeping shadow of the AIDS crisis has made things a thousand times worse.

On the morning of that first day we were to visit an AIDS victim. Thom Kasuba and a group of ladies known as the Community Based Home Care Team were to accompany us. The Community Based Home Care Team is a Catholic initiative supported by World Vision and headed by Phyllis Chintu, a trained nurse who teaches and leads her dedicated, inadequately equipped team with quiet competence and great charm. A big blue box of medicines accompanies the team wherever they go, but, Phyllis told us ruefully, the contents are severely limited.

There was no sign of the person we had come to visit when we arrived at the poorly roofed, tumbledown house. Ladies from the team fetched chairs from inside and set them in a line for us visitors to use. They brought out a rough blanket and laid it on the gritty yellow earth at our feet. Two of the ladies then re-entered and emerged from the dark interior seconds later supporting a frail, unsteady figure. They sat her carefully down on the blanket in front of us and stepped back. So. Here was an AIDS sufferer for us to meet. Here was a specimen. Here was a human being, a woman in her thirties, who was unlikely to live for very much longer because the plague that is tearing Africa apart is lodged in her body and there are no drugs available for her to take – certainly not in the blue box that has been laid so carefully on the chair at the end of the row. The team will wash her, and try to treat her immediate symptoms, and offer her words of comfort and care, but the sentence is irrevocable. Rois will surely die.

There is a scream beginning somewhere deep inside me. It grows and rises. I have to choke it before it can emerge into the dry air of Zamtan. I am not here to scream. Rois is crying. Tears are running down her cheeks. Why is she crying? Does she always cry? Oh, God, does she sit in the gloomy darkness of that ruin of a house of hers and cry all through the day for what she has already lost and what she is inevitably going to lose?

No, she is not crying, Phyllis tells us. It is an eye condition. Her system is so weak that any infection can attack her.

Well, what is that strange encrustation on the skin that is visible beneath her flimsy gold-coloured blouse?

That is shingles. Rois suffers from shingles. It is a painful, uncomfortable condition.

AIDS. Shingles. Death. Where is my faith? I manage to control my face, but there is a panic growing in me. I scrabble around in my heart and mind searching for my faith. There seems to be a vacuum in the space where my beliefs have always been. The power is gone. The power is off. I remember our little set of plug sockets. Yes, that is it. There is nowhere in this poverty-stricken, disease-ridden place for me to plug my faith in. It is faith born and nurtured in a land where food is always plentiful and medicine is always available, where we have the luxury of sitting in well-fed groups tearing Bible verses apart and telling each other that we think the Lord might possibly be saying something or other to somebody or other about some trivial issue that will never significantly affect anyone anyway. Rois, I have nothing for you. Everything that meant so much to me has gone. The power has gone and I have not the slightest idea how to reconnect and replenish it.

I would sob, but Bridget and I are not here to sob. We are here to observe and make notes and eventually write a book that might actually help people like Rois in the future. We are here to learn that James, the brother of Jesus, was right when he said that true religion is to help widows and orphans and stay unpolluted by the world.

Plug into that, says God, and I'll sort the power out.

The rhythm of hope

B: What is Zamtan? What is its history? Why have communities like this become such black spots for AIDS? The answers are tragic.

Located in the Copperbelt province in north-eastern Zambia, the community of Zamtan is situated 12 miles south-east of Kitwe, the second largest city in Zambia. Originally Zamtan, together with the neighbouring villages of Zambia and Kokolo, formed a transit town with makeshift shelters. Truckers employed by the Zambia-Tanzania Transport Company would stop over here for a day or two while they loaded up and unloaded at the nearby copper mine.

Then, overnight, the company collapsed and the truckers were stranded. Some of them were thousands of miles away from their homes with no means of returning. They stayed, and the shanty town became their permanent home – even though less than one per cent of the population actually owned the land on which their makeshift shelters were built. They could not afford improvements to their shacks, and as a result many houses have collapsed over the years and most of those still standing are in an appalling state of disrepair. All of the truckers who happened to be bunking down in Zamtan on that fateful day decades ago were abruptly deprived of an income, with little chance of finding work, however hard they tried. Even those lucky enough to find 'piece work' in the nearby town as house boys or casual labourers on construction sites could not earn more than about £10 a month, a wage way below subsistence level. The situation never improved. There are very few jobs to be had.

The men married women from surrounding villages, settled down and had children. These families are even now subsisting on less than fifty pence a day. The sparse, scrubby landscape reflects this widespread and devastating poverty. There are no trees. They have all been chopped down for house repairs or fires. Without shade there is no vegetation, there are no crops and never any spare money to plough into development.

But an even deadlier killer than starvation was lurking, ready to strike.

The truckers had often had to live away from home for many months, and many of them had sought comfort and sex with prostitutes. As a result of these sexual encounters, a large number had become unsuspecting carriers of HIV/AIDS. Twenty years ago the virus had not yet been identified. Although the virus was isolated in 1983, it was only several years later that researchers discovered that the disease is transmitted from person to person. By this time it was too late. The disease had spread like a forest fire among wives, and then from mothers to children. As these children grew up, took partners and became parents, the fire raged ever more out of control. People were dying, and mortality due to HIV/AIDS-related illnesses has continued unabated to the present day.

As poverty deepened, nutrition deteriorated, the death toll increased and emotional trauma abounded, it became terrifyingly clear to the citizens of Zamtan, Zambia and Kokola that HIV/AIDS was decimating their communities. The stench of stigma and fear and denial was everywhere. Defeat and despair prevailed, and it seemed that death had the victory.

Then, one by one, aid agencies, including World Vision, started to get involved. Under the charismatic leadership of Fordson Kafwetu, with the support of many energetic members of the community, something very exciting began to evolve. This development would dramatically change the atmosphere in this desperate little corner of Zambia.

The AIDS-related projects are an integral part of a bigger programme designed to improve the lives of Zamtan's residents. The bigger programme – called an Area Development Programme – covers important things like improving the supply and quality of water in the community, improving education standards and opportunities, providing basic health services and running vocational training courses. Most of this is paid for and supported by World Vision child sponsors in the USA.

People are still dying of AIDS, of course. At the time of our visit, out of a combined population of seventeen thousand for the three communities, one thousand were already orphans. On average, one adult or child dies every month. But an explosion of ideas and creativity has replaced the lethargy and despair. Tentatively at first, but with increasing confidence, the people have begun to dance – to a rhythm of positive living. A rhythm of hope and eventual resurrection.

2. Orphans and Angels

B: We had known from the outset of our trip that we would be meeting orphans. Unavoidable in a community where the average life expectancy is thirty-five years and where a generation of adults is being decimated by the killer AIDS. Knowing in advance does not do much to lessen the shock when you encounter the effects of this pandemic face to face, as we discovered when we met Lackson Banda and Philemon (pronounced 'Filly-mon') Lackson, brothers who lost both parents to the disease when they were very young.

The boys are waiting for us. The ground in front of their home has been carefully swept. Three chairs have been placed in a row facing their front entrance, one of them, judging from its precarious list to the left, for decorative purposes only. That leaves two. One for Adrian and one for me. We sit. The boys stand closely together, a fragile wall of defence, staring at us incuriously as we ask our silly questions. Two largish white people, each armed with a little notebook and a pen. What have we to do with their world? Their faces are blank. The impression is that they are enduring an ordeal which must eventually end.

Philemon, the younger brother, is barefoot, dusty but clean. He is clearly anxious, head down, self-consciously fixing his eyes on a patch of ground to his left. His tee shirt hangs loosely on his skinny frame, holes and faded cotton in equal proportions. While patently longing for this inexplicable encounter to be over he does not shuffle or shift. He endures, waits, expects nothing, relying on his brother to take the lead – as he has probably done for the last four years. Lackson, on the other hand, meets our eyes calmly, his head held high, and, despite being slight for his age, there is dignity in his bearing. We notice a watch on his wrist. A gift? An heirloom? Does it work? He has the aura of the survivor, wiry, defiant, self-sufficient. His shorts may be frayed, and his broken, gaping, lace-less shoes may cling by sheer will-power to his dusty feet, but he is the provider, the protector, the head of the family. He is fourteen years old.

Thom Kasuba, our guide for today, speaks gently to the boys. They visibly relax and sit, leaning against the sun-warmed wall of their home. Lackson stretches his gangly teenage limbs in front of him. Philemon is cross-legged, his eyes still averted, head down. 'Just put up with it,' I can feel him thinking, 'it will be over soon.'

A young woman dressed in a checked blouse and bright skirt steps forward to talk to the boys. We recognize her from an earlier community meeting. Thom explains that Agnes is their caregiver. She visits the boys regularly. We already know a little about the Caregivers. Originally they had been furnished with the rather unrealistic title 'Guardian Angels'. We smiled when we learned that World Vision had provided 43 bicycles to make it possible for them to reach those they served, needy people whose homes are scattered around the

community. Guardian Angels on bicycles. The concept
had seemed rather sweet and endearing at the time,
slightly unreal. Now I watch Philemon disappearing
eagerly through the front door of his home to emerge
seconds later with a sliced open maize bag which he
carefully places on the ground for his friend to sit on.
There is no physical contact, but I am relieved to sense a
comfortable familiarity between them as they sit
together.

I whisper to Thom, "They look as if they enjoy Agnes
coming."

"They do."

"What does she bring them?"

"She brings them spiritual counselling."

My mind whirls. She brings them what? Spiritual
counselling? Nothing else? No food? No blankets? No
clothes? No toys? No money? Even I can see that their
roof is falling to pieces. And it's their winter, for goodness
sake, with temperatures dropping at night to near
freezing. I decide maybe I had misheard him as I watch
the three of them talking, and I resolve to question Thom
further about it. I notice that Lackson has got an ugly bite
on his cheek and I long to dress it for him. Embarrassed
by my response, I turn my attention to my surroundings.
The ground in front of the dwelling has been meticulous-
ly swept. A scrap of corrugated iron from the dis-
integrating roof and a triangle of ash-covered stones
mark out their cooking area. Other boulders secure what
is left of the roof. There is nothing else to distract me.
There is nothing else here. Reluctantly, I look back at the
boys, hating my inadequacy, yearning to dispel the
horrible fear that we are merely an audience, and, from
their point of view, potentially a hostile one.

At last. Adrian is asking a question.

"Would you like to tell us your story?"

Philemon immediately averts his eyes. It is going to be up to Lackson. He does not fail. His eyes meet ours determinedly.

"Our mother died four years ago. Our father was already dead. They died from HIV/AIDS. Our grandmother came. It was not good. Now she has gone. She has gone to live on a farm in the bush."

That's it?

I quickly scramble these scraps of facts together. By ages ten and nine these little boys had lost both their parents. But they had a grandmother. She came. A year later she had gone and they were alone.

"Why – why did she go?"

Lackson's confidence suddenly falters. He looks very vulnerable. His eyes look down, the fragile strand of communication between us broken. Something is badly wrong. His voice, when it comes, is small.

"She wanted to go to the bush."

"Why did you not go with her?"

Another pause.

"She was troubling us."

Troubling you?

"And we wanted to go to school. So we stay in our home. We stay here."

His head is up again. His eyes again meet ours. He is back in control. The danger is over, but there is a need in Adrian and I to press him on how two boys of eleven and ten could possibly survive on their own.

"So how – I mean, who cooks for you?"

"I cook. My mother was very sick before she died. I learnt to cook then."

"What do you eat?"

"Rats. It is rats we eat."

Rats? Did he say rats? Just when I thought I was on safe ground.

"We have traps."

Lackson turns to his brother. There is a swift exchange of words. Philemon shoots off into the house and returns with two home-made traps. He holds one of them out silently on his flat, outstretched hand. Lackson speaks with a new confidence. Here is something practical that he really knows about.

"We go out early into the bush. We can catch twenty, thirty in a day. We keep some for relish with our *nshima*."

Adrian and I look at each other and nod. Something we know about at last. *Nshima*, a staple of the diet in this area, is a thick white porridge made from maize flour and water.

"The rest of the rats we sell."

"How much do you make for each rat?"

Am I really asking this?

Lackson's reply is animated. He obviously takes a pride in his ability as a salesman.

"Two hundred kwacha a rat. (2 pence?) We can buy our maize with this money."

He smiles a rare smile. His teeth gleam. No work for orthodontists over here. Perhaps rats'n'maize is a dish we need in the West.

"If we could find enough rats maybe for 5,000 kwacha, we could buy some second-hand clothes."

He shrugs, grinning at the absurdity of his dream. The equivalent of £2. Riches beyond avarice!

Drowning in our reactions, we clutch at the branch used by generations of adults who have run out of things to say to children. School.

"You say you stayed because you wanted to go to school. What is your favourite subject?"

Philemon whispers his shyly.

"Mathematics. Bemba (the vernacular language of the area). And English."

Lackson's eyes are bright, his face suddenly animated and now completely free from suspicion. "Science is mine. We're learning how the sun comes out and creates days equal in length – and geography – I really like geography."

Time for one last absurd question.

"And what do you want to be when you grow up?"

Lackson's reply comes instantly, with Philemon's straight on its tail. Evidence of long night-time conversations in the cold blackness of their small damp bedroom area.

"A pilot!"

"A policeman!"

Oh, Lackson Banda and Philemon Lackson. Of course that's what you dream of being. Shiny hats. Smart uniforms. Polished black shoes. Not to mention the pristine shirts, clean underpants and socks and gleaming badges. Perhaps more importantly, a sense of belonging, of being someone special.

A quick tour of the dark interior with the boys as our guides, confirms what we already knew. They are very poor. A small rickety stand displays one saucepan, one bowl, one plastic mug, a box of matches and two somewhat tatty school books. A string, stretched across the corner from two nails, sports another pair of disreputable shorts and a couple of ragged shirts, completing the boys' wardrobe. No bed. No blanket. No mosquito net. No light.

Blinking as we emerge into the startling sunshine, we stand in an uneasy group. The boys have switched off, their task as informants and guides over. We shake hands. We leave. I am walking next to Thom.

"How is it that the Caregivers bring them so little?"

Thom looks surprised.

"Oh, but they do," he reiterates, "they bring comfort and friendship. They share the gospel with them."

I feel embarrassed that I had not valued the gift of spiritual encouragement.

"Yes, but what about material needs? Their roof has holes. They are hungry. They have no clothes. They don't even have blankets. They ..."

"They are not vulnerable enough," Thom explains in his solemn way. "You have seen how well they are coping. They are very self-sufficient. Until we have many more sponsors they will not receive much more help. There are so many who are so much worse."

Worse? Surely it is enough to have lost both parents before even reaching your teenage years. Surely no child should be forced to go rat-catching before school in order to stay alive. Surely boys of this age should not be soaked in the rainy season through a leaking roof, and frozen on winter nights because of having no blanket. Things must change. And they will, if more and more children like these are sponsored by those of us who have no need to revert to a rodent diet.

Guardian angels

B: During our time in Zamtan we met several caregivers like Agnes. What particularly struck both of us was their selflessness. Churches select both women and men from their congregations to do this volunteer work. While most of them care for orphans in their own homes, they are also often called out at night and frequently asked to delve into their own pockets.

A caregiver called Loveness told a story I especially liked. Loveness came upon a very sick lady who had not eaten anything for three days because she had completely run out of food. What could she do? Loveness went home, took a bowl and did the rounds of all her neighbours, asking if they could spare just a little pinch of maize so that between them all there would be enough for a meal to feed the lady in her care.

A caregiver called David told of how he came across a 'certain young girl called Margaret with a sore lower limb'. He took the ten-year-old child to the clinic and was asked to pay the consultant's fees. He tried to persuade the medical officer that the child was an orphan and there was no one to pay the fees, but he was told that it was clinic policy that all should contribute. What could he do? Only one thing. Use money he had for his own family. He gave this to the clinic, and the child was cured.

Gently spoken Emmanuel is responsible for five children of his own and four of his elder brother's children, in addition to his full-time volunteer work, visiting and helping the extremely sick in his village. I can still see the sad resignation in his eyes as he told us, "I do not have time to work, but the Catholic diocese gives me a bag of maize a month. Sadly it does not last us so very long, but we are grateful."

Perhaps the caregiver that made the most lasting impression on us was Femmy Ngoma – confident, physically strong and immensely likeable. On our first day in Zamtan we met a very ill young widow who told us that she regarded this wonderful caregiver as her mother. We saw Femmy later that day with a family of newly orphaned children, and I wondered how they saw her role in their lives.

Kelvin Chisanga was the youngest of these orphans, and we have to confess that he never said a single word to us. But his huge anxious eyes told us that, at two years old, he had known more than his fair share of troubles. We pieced together information gathered from his brothers and sisters and carers involved with the family. Here is Kelvin's story as he might have told it:

Inside Kelvin

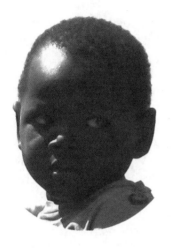

My name is Kelvin. I am two years old. I am a very sad boy. My grown-up friend Femmy says it is all right to be very sad. That is because a very sad thing happened in our family.

Three weeks ago we were all asleep in our house. I woke up because I was shivery with cold and heard a funny noise. The noise was my big sister, Nalisa. She was crying. I went to her and climbed onto her lap. She told me that she was going to look after me now. Then in the morning they took me to the house next door and I had to stay there all day and when I came back home Mummy was not at our house any more. I never saw her again after that night when Nalisa cried.

I knew that my mummy was very sick. Every day ladies in green dresses with red bows came to see her. They came in the morning to give her a nice wash. They brought her special food to make her strong, like tiny fish and soya. Sometimes the ladies looked very sad. That made me feel frightened. They had a big blue box with a handle and I liked watching them open it and take out things. It was full of little white boxes with lids on. The little boxes had lots of pills inside. They told me the pills were to help our mummy not to feel so sick.

One day my big brother Dyness, who is eight, asked them if the pills would make Mummy better. They told us to go and play. We knew Mummy was very ill because she could not get up to make our porridge any more. So Nalisa started making our porridge when she came home from school. She still makes our porridge. When Mummy made our porridge there were some vegetables with it, but usually now it is just porridge. Ridia, who is twelve, makes the fire. He wants to be a driver and a mechanic when he grows up, so he says he is good at fires. No one makes us any breakfast, but we haven't had breakfast since our daddy died. We get a bit hungry. I have another very big brother. He is eighteen. He is at school too. His name is Ramec. He is very grown up when he talks. He says he is studying for the future so he can look after us all. I don't know what he means. I have heard of being a mechanic and a driver but the future must be a very grand job because Ramec works very hard. When the others are at school the lady who lives in the house next to us looks after Dyness and me. She does not have any food to give us because she says she has not got enough for her own family. But my big friend Femmy sometimes gives us a potato she has cooked.

I'd like to tell you about my big friend Femmy. Nalisa says Femmy is called a Guardian Angel. Femmy laughed a lot when I asked her if she was one. She said that they used to be called Guardian Angels but they did not feel they were special enough to be called that so now they are called Caregivers. I am glad. I think Femmy's teeth are too big to be an angel's teeth and she always wears a funny scarf tied on top of her head, but she has a big, big smile which makes me feel safe so maybe she is one really. Dyness says she is like our *goma* (grandmother). I think she is our special friend. She lives very near to us so we see her a lot.

When Femmy comes we can cuddle up on her big lap and she tells us stories about Jesus. She says Mummy lives with Jesus now. I wish she still lived with us but I try not to keep saying it because it makes Nalisa cry. Nalisa says she wants to be a nurse when she grows up so she can help make people like our mummy better. She says

Mummy had an illness called TB. I asked her if TB is dirty and makes people who play with people die. She got cross and went away and I saw her crying so I didn't ask her any more. But there is a boy who lives near us and he says his mummy says he can't play with us any more. He calls me names. He says I am some more letters but I can't remember which ones. I know they are not T and B. He says they make me dirty and will make him die if I play with him and touch him by mistake. Ramec has told him that is silly but he still isn't allowed to play with me.

Sometimes Femmy brings us things and tells us about some other friends we have never met. We have their pictures in our house. They don't look like us at all. They help us a lot. They live in a country called America. Femmy says it is because four of us have these special friends that we all have blankets in our house. So that is why the lady who looks after Dyness and me has not got blankets for all her children. Because they have not got pictures in their house. Femmy says they send money every month and because they do Ramec and Nalisa and Ridia can go to school. The people who live in America pay for their school money and for their books and their uniforms. That is why Ramec can study for the future and Ridia can be a mechanic when he grows up. And there is another very good thing. Because we have these friends we are going to have our roof made better so that when it rains we will not get wet. I know that is very important. The ladies in the green dresses with red bows used to get cross when they came to see Mummy and she was wet from the rain which came through all the holes. They would go and get friends to put big stones on the roof to keep the tin pieces on it. So I know a new roof is good. Maybe when we have a new roof Nalisa will smile again. She is very pretty. I think she looks more like an angel than Femmy, but don't tell anyone I said that.

Unconscious art?

A: "What on earth is all that noise about?"

I put this question to Thom, our guide and companion, as we strolled along one of the sear and dusty pathways of Zamtan on our way to meet one of the families regularly visited by the Caregivers. It was a lovely morning. In fact, Bridget and I reckoned that the weather on that Thursday was just about perfect, approximating to what we in England like to call a beautiful summer's day. Many Zambians would have smiled and shivered and disagreed with our view of the weather. As far as they were concerned it was the middle of winter, and distinctly on the chilly side. We had been amazed to learn that, even in the middle of winter, Thom was in the habit of taking a cold bath every morning, because, he said, it was a 'good way to start the day'.

As we walked, the hush of our straw-coloured, scrubby surroundings had been abruptly shattered by a loud, hectoring voice, its artificial enhancement strangely at variance with the very basic, non-electrical ethos of Zamtan.

After I asked my question we all stopped and turned to look along the path in the direction that we had just come from. The source of the noise was walking steadily along the path behind us. It was a woman. She was dressed in blue sandals, a long colourful skirt patterned in blue, red and green, a light blue top buttoned under the neck, and a woollen hat fitting closely to her head. A large yellow plastic container with a red screw cap hung from her left hand, while with her right she clutched the handle of a battery-powered megaphone, the device that Americans call a 'bullhorn'. It was from this instrument, held near to her mouth, that all the sounds were emerging. Whatever it was that this lady was so anxious to communicate, there could be no denying the energy and enthusiasm with which she was doing it. She meant every loud, metallic, amplified word. She was not speaking in English, however. I modified my question.

"What is that lady saying?"

A small smile deepened the creases in Thom's customarily serious face as he replied.

"Oh, she is calling people out to bring water to help with the brick-making," he explained.

"Is that all she's saying?"

He shook his head and broke into a throaty chuckle.

"Oh, no, that is not all! She is saying to people that they are quick enough to come out when the G.I.K.'s arrive – "

"G.I.K.'s?"

"Yes, G.I.K.'s. It means 'Gifts In Kind'. Sometimes gifts come to the community in the form of food or blankets or clothes. This lady is saying that everyone hurries out to take their share of the G.I.K.'s when they arrive, and she thinks they should be just as quick to come and help when a job has to be done."

"I see."

I looked at the lady in the coloured skirt with renewed interest. There was something rather magnificent about the unconscious theatricality with which she boldly broadcasted her acerbic message to the local residents. A rare touch of satire perhaps. A happening. A handsome piece of living art. A dead cert for the Zamtan equivalent of the Turner Prize if such a thing were to be offered – especially in a community where there are few if any beds to unmake, where no one could ever afford to waste a whole cow by cutting it in half for an art exhibit, and where screwed-up sheets of paper are heavily in demand for makeshift footballs.

Would you vote for her? I would.

The little girl in the pink frilly dress

A: We meet a little girl in a pink frilly dress, but we know almost nothing about her.

What do we know? Well, she has a pink frilly dress on. Yes, okay, we know that. It sits rather oddly on her still, small body, like a party frock worn by mistake, too late and on the wrong day, and then allowed to stay on because it is the only element of the party that has survived.

We might even be able to have a stab at her name. I glance at my notebook, the one that will go everywhere with me in Zambia, and I see that she is one of three children. But which one? She must be Aston Sondashi, Lister Chola or Frances Chanda. I think Aston is a boy's name, so the little girl in the pink frilly dress must be either Lister Chola or Frances Chanda. I want her to be called Lister because I think that is a prettier name, but it is no more than a guess. How old is she? Four? No more than four, surely.

What else do we know about the little girl in the pink frilly dress? She has quite a bad cold. Her nose is running straight down into her mouth, and neither she nor anyone else seems to be in any hurry to wipe her face clean. There is a suggestion of bruising around and beneath her eyes – not the kind of bruising that results from physical cruelty, but perhaps rather a symptom of impending problems with her sight.

The little girl in the pink frilly dress is covered by a layer or layers of Zamtan dust, perhaps the dust of many days, or even weeks. I am quite sure, as we stand and look at this tiny squidge of humanity, that Bridget will be filled with a yearning to whisk her away and put her in a shower, and find a new, clean dress for her to wear while the other one is being washed, and get someone to take a look at those eyes, and play a few silly games at the kitchen table, and work towards the possibility of a real smile appearing on those curiously intense, slightly puzzled features.

Yes, the little girl in the pink frilly dress does have an air of puzzlement about her, a sense of sustained shock, as though her brief encounter with life has been a slow-motion smack in the face. Sun, stone, dust and a fading pink frilly dress are the constants in her life. She stares uncomprehendingly into the camera. What is that thing? Why is it pointing at her? Does it mean something? Will it give her anything? Who are these people with the funny pale skin who wear lots of clothes?

We do know that the little girl in the pink frilly dress has a mother and a father. They are introduced to us by the Caregivers on this startling first day in Zamtan.

For both Bridget and me the encounter is like a clump round the head with a wooden cudgel. We are invited to sit on a bench outside their apology for a house. They sit opposite us. We look at them, but it is a second or two before we register the fact that they are not seeing us. How could they? They are blind. Nobody told us in advance that both of them are blind.

Why does this first meeting hit us so very hard? Perhaps it is because these trips to the most impoverished parts of countries in the developing world involve a dislocation or readjustment of perspectives and values that, by their very nature, simply cannot happen gently. The contrast is too great. For us, the collision between our cushioned world and their stark existence is a bit of a train crash. We manage to pull ourselves together. We have to. Having our notebooks and pens makes us feel slightly better, partly, I suspect, because they are like badges of qualification, suggesting to us, if to no one else, that we do actually have a function in this place. We ask some questions.

How do they live?

They live by buying and selling small quantities of vegetables. Spread out on two empty meal sacks in front of them are five or six small piles of sweet potatoes. How much profit can remain at this lowest-of-all stage in the chain of transactions? They tell us that a Catholic aid organization sometimes provides them with maize meal to make *nshima*.

What do the Caregivers do for them?

The Caregivers are unable to provide material help because their resources are so scarce, but they do offer spiritual encouragement. The parents of the little girl in the pink frilly dress tell us that their happiest times are when they are able to share the gospel and pray with the men and women who visit them.

What about the future?

We must move forward with Jesus, they tell us. One day he will come back and everything will be all right.

As we ask our questions and listen to their answers we are continually interrupted by a wild figure who has been sitting with our little group outside the house since we first arrived. He is thin, ragged and frantic of eye. Agitated and emotional, he gesticulates crazily from his seat on the ground beside the blind couple, shouting and groaning and raving about the constant hunger that everyone is experiencing, the need for more food, for enough food, for some food. He does not seem to find any comfort in the prospect of Jesus returning one day. He just wants to eat. One or two of the Caregivers remonstrate gently with him, explaining that he must not interrupt and make a noise because these people have come a long way, all the way from England in fact, to find out what is needed in Zambia. They will go home and tell folk in their own country and then perhaps more help will come. The Caregivers obviously consider this man to be somewhat deranged. Perhaps he is. But, as we are to discover more and more in our travels through Zamtan, he is actually like a secular prophet of the people, unrestrainedly expressing the need that aches and grinds through the daily lives of thousands.

"More food. More food, please. Whatever else we may need or ultimately benefit from – just now, right now, at this moment in our lives, we must have more food, because, you see, we are so very, very hungry."

I consider the fact that Jesus understands completely. He knew and knows all about food. He says that when he knocks on the door and we choose to open it he will come in and eat with us. The parents of the little girl in the pink frilly dress would like to have a little more to offer him than is in their house at present. I feel quite sure that when the master does return he would much rather find people eating well than dying of starvation. And that, I realize yet again, is up to us. He can make it possible if we will help.

When our meeting ends we rise awkwardly to our feet, close our notebooks and prepare to leave. The little girl in the pink frilly dress stands against a crumbling brick wall and stares at us. Her mother and father have never seen her. They have no way of knowing that her nose needs wiping. Cleaning the dust from her body is not – simply cannot be – a priority in their lives. They have five children, and she is just one of them. For this family, shares in everything are very small.

So, little girl in the pink frilly dress, possibly Lister, so pretty underneath the dust and the snot, we have to leave you now, just as poor as you were when we arrived. You are not terribly important to anyone, are you? Nevertheless, you may be surprised to hear that you have an important job to do for us and for many other people who live in places like this. Look steadily out of your picture at all the people who are reading about you now, and say to them that a little assistance would be much

appreciated if they would be so kind. If they read and respond to the plea that is written on your puzzled face you will have done very, very well. Thank you on behalf of all the people who will be helped just because of you, and on behalf of Jesus himself.

Please pray for the little girl in the pink frilly dress.

3. Window of Hope

B: Every day in Zambia brought its surprises, but none more than the half-hour Adrian and I spent squashed into tiny desks in a classroom at Welbeck junior school. Having watched a dance performed by exquisite small girls with accompanying scissor-like hand actions, we asked our interpreter what the song meant.

"Oh they are singing about castrating the rapist," was the calm reply.

"*Vitendendi:* Cut, cut!"

"Sorry?"

"If you are not sexually controlled we will cut you off. Cut, cut!"

We marvelled yet again at the extraordinary leap that people here have had to make from being part of a society in which talk of sex and death was absolutely taboo, to one whose very survival depends on unsentimental utterances such as these. Clearly, childish innocence and ignorance, even in warriors this young, are considered to no longer have a place.

But it was what followed that surprised me even more. Two young boys approached the front of the classroom and took up positions on either side of the blackboard. One of the boys stuck a large sheet of paper covered with writing onto the board while the other quelled any would-be rebels with a steely gaze. Adrian and I instinctively sat up straighter. Using a ruler to emphasize their points the two boys proceeded to deliver an informed exposition on their chosen subject. It was the sort of presentation that is encouraged in many a classroom, but the subject was not the growth of the runner bean or the characteristics of marsupials. It was, yes, you've guessed it, HIV/AIDS and how not to catch it.

In confident staccato English our young experts took it in turns to tell us:

"HIV/AIDS is spread by sexual intercourse.

By blood transfusion.

By shared needles.

By re-used or non-sterilized needles, blades or surgical gloves in poorly resourced hospitals.

By mother to child infection.

By breastfeeding.

And that, (this bit in unison) is how it is spread."

With a small bow they returned modestly to their seats, to rapturous applause from their classmates. It seemed so clinical, these coldly adult facts expressed in voices that weren't likely to break for several more years. But we should not have been surprised. We were, after all, attending a meeting of the regularly held school AIDS club. Similar clubs are springing up in every school in the land. The age range between five and fifteen has been dubbed the 'Window of Hope'. Children between these ages are considered old enough to begin to understand the risks, but they are not yet widely exposed to the dangers connected with sexual activity. Teachers are therefore being trained in all aspects of prevention. Staff have been encouraged not only to bring the subject into the curriculum, but also to use it as a basis for dance, drama and song.

Earlier in the week we had attended an annual World Vision outdoor drama and singing competition between several school AIDS clubs. We had witnessed some really imaginative explorations of the theme, all performed with startling energy and confidence by children between the ages of eight and fifteen. Teachers had made the most of the opportunity to extend the children's use of the English language, which made the event more relevant and exciting for us.

In one of the dramas a boy was holding a football. He tried to persuade several other children to join in with his game. The children passed the ball along the line chanting in unison:

"AIDS is like a football.

It goes to that one and to that one."

The leader then took possession of the ball and tried to pass it to each of the children in turn. One by one they handed it back, declaring their reasons for refusing to play.

"No I do not want to play this game."

"It is a dangerous game."

"I say no to casual sex."

"It can cost your life."

Another poem which remains in my memory began with the chorus stepping forward and shouting:

"CON-FU-SION!"

Then, one by one, the children, none of whom appeared to be more than about ten, stepped forward with a single, explosively delivered line, accompanied by an action which they then froze. It was difficult to catch all of these lines, mainly because of the enthusiastic audience participation, but it went something like this:

"HIV – what it is
A condition
HIV is a virus
It destroys the body's immune system
It causes diarrhoea
CON-FU-SION!
I am an orphan
Back away
I am a widow
Back away
How did it start?
That is not important for us to know
How can I protect myself?
Abstain
Stick to one sexual partner.
If we don't fight together
We won't defeat it."

And this one:

"AIDS
I hate you
You are rotten
You smell bad
You reach the highest mountain of the world
Who can save us?
We know how happy you become

> When you enter the body's immune system
> But you are fighting a losing battle.
> We will defeat you."

Robert, the teacher who organized this particular event, is a peripatetic drama teacher. He is one of those born educators who clearly loves his job. His role is to help the children express themselves confidently. In addition to being in charge of the proceedings, he also took parts in some of the sketches. Unfortunately they were in Bemba, so we were not able to understand them. Judging by the howls of laughter from the packed audience of children from various schools in the area, they were very funny – especially the one where Robert pretended to be an angry, screaming, kicking toddler with his thumb in his mouth being told off by his mother, a girl of about fourteen. Despite the fact that the message was serious and explicit, the atmosphere of the whole event was one of warmth, fun and creativity. Perhaps humour is a key to eliciting responses from this vitally important age group. Or perhaps Zambians simply love to laugh and sing and dance and are naturally very creative. Probably both.

Having been educated by our two junior lecturers, and having absorbed the message from more than twenty songs and dramas, I am inspired to dig out a few more facts and pass them on to you.

What is AIDS?

Acquired immuno-deficiency syndrome (AIDS) is the end result of most cases of HIV infection.

HIV (the human immunodeficiency virus) progressively damages the immune system, preventing the body from protecting itself against infection.

AIDS does not kill straight away. From the time of infection a person may live in good health for two to ten years, yet once infected even someone with no symptoms will still be able to transmit the virus to others.

A number of antiviral agents and treatments have been developed to prolong the lives of people with AIDS, but no effective vaccine or cure has yet been found.

Frightening, relevant, sobering statistics

- Around forty million adults and children live with HIV/AIDS.
- Ninety-five per cent of these live in underdeveloped countries, with over two-thirds (28 million) living in Africa.
- Twenty-one million people have already died of AIDS – more than lost their lives as a result of bubonic plague.
- By 2005, one hundred million people will have been infected by AIDS – more than the combined casualties, military and civilian, of World Wars I and II.
- By 2010, forty million children will have been orphaned by AIDS.
- Life expectancy in Zambia is thirty-five years.

So, there we have it. Amidst these overwhelming statistics, the following line from one of the children's songs struck both Adrian and me and has come back again and again to haunt us:

"We never died like this before ..."

Neither cowed nor bowed

A: "Some paper has come. I thought I would bring it to you."

Joyce Nonde thanks the young teacher who has just entered her office, and regards the packet of plain A4 paper as if it were made of gold. She lays it gently on the desk in front of her.

Those who complain of poor funding in schools in the United Kingdom would do well to visit Kamfinsa School, located within the World Vision development project in Zamtan. Joyce has been the headmistress here for three years, earning 400,000 kwacha (about £50) a month. She is, to say the least, a force. She needs to be. We sit on the big plumpy sofa that fills up half of her tiny, makeshift office, listening as she explains some of the problems that she faces in trying to make a difference in the lives of the pupils in her care.

"We have seven hundred children attending the school every day, many of them setting off from home at 5:30 in the morning and walking up to nine kilometres in order to get here. Most of the children are orphans, cared for by grandparents who find it hard to scrape together enough food for one simple meal a day, let alone provide a school lunch. I have eight teachers working for me, which means that each class contains around ninety children, and we have no facilities for feeding the children during the day. The younger ones finish their school day much earlier than the older ones. This means that they have to wait hours for big brothers or sisters to finish before they can set off on the long trek home. And yet they come. There is a school for them, you see, and so they come."

The financial constraints of the establishment are somehow encapsulated in the significance that Joyce attaches to the arrival of this simple pack of white paper, brought into the office by a smart-looking male teacher. Bridget and I stare thoughtfully at this slim provision. It is a little embarrassing. We go through packs like this at a rate of knots, and there are only two of us, not seven hundred.

Joyce seems neither cowed nor bowed by the difficulties that she faces. She is doing the job, and she is doing it with fierce determination. She knows most of her seven hundred children by name, and when something needs to happen she will move mountains to make it possible.

"Sometimes," she says, "a child will be taken sick and have to go to hospital. In a case like that I have quite often had to use my own money. There is no choice. I wish that we could have our own bus and driver so that the children would not have to walk such a long way to school." She shakes her head ruefully. "But it is so much money. Even better would be if this was a boarding school so that some of the pupils could stay and be looked after during the week."

It is at this moment that she becomes aware of the young teacher still hovering by the door.

"Excuse me, but I just wondered if I might have two sheets of the new paper for the debate, you know."

We watch in silence as she carefully removes two sheets from the new pack and gives them to him. He hurries off instantly to deploy his resources while we get back to the subject in hand.

"Tell us about the AIDS work that you do here."

"As well as the curriculum," she replies, gesturing towards a large complicated chart on the wall behind her, "we run choirs, drama teams and workshops for the children that are all connected with AIDS education. I really do believe that my students need to be given accurate information about this deadly virus, so that they can support each other when there is a need to avoid high-risk situations later on."

The debate

And that is our main reason for being here today. Today, two of the local schools have assembled at Kamfinsa to stage a debate, supported and opposed by the children themselves, in which the motion will be that 'men alone are to blame for the spread of AIDS'. As we enter and take our seats at school desks especially imported for our use, we see that the two sheets of paper are already fulfilling their destiny. Stuck with Sellotape to the front of the stage, they inform us of the names of the two schools that have won places in the final: Cedrics and Kamfinsa.

Hundreds of children have gathered in the surprisingly vast school hall, the active participators in seats near the front, with a seething mass of non-participating, mainly younger audience members crushed into the large space at the back. The debate turns out to be an impressively formal affair, involving children of all ages and sizes mounting the stage, bowing to judges and audience, and loudly declaiming speeches ("Before I elaborate" is a favourite phrase) that have been learned by heart. It is all done with great verve and aplomb. Older teenagers are heavily involved, but in some cases the voice is definitely quite a bit larger than the debater.

"Men are to blame," one tiny lad named Herbert roars with total confidence, "they take advantage of the desire of women to be married."

"But," replies one opposing the motion, "a man is like a lion hunting for impala, and women are like impala. They are taught how to be attractive to the opposite sex, so they are to blame."

Not an easy argument to follow, this last one.

As in all schools, one or two of the children suffer a memory loss when their big moment finally arrives, but the onlookers respond sympathetically to failure and enthusiastically to everything else.

The debate is long, good-humoured and very equally argued, but in the end the motion is carried. 'Men alone are to blame for the spread of AIDS.' Whether this is a fair conclusion is beyond the power of my wit and wisdom to decide, but I am aware that in the course of planning and rehearsing for this event the children involved have been forced to confront and think through many issues that will have a direct effect on their lives.

Today's presentation also includes some of the songs and poems that we have already heard elsewhere. One or two of the songs performed by one choir in particular seem to enter into the very centre of our hearts and minds.

What is it about these African harmonies and those who produce them? I sit and listen, totally entranced, searching within myself for words that will begin to express how they make me feel. Perhaps the music that these young people are producing is like a forest of startling, multi-coloured blooms erupting from the dry earth, a triumph of life and freshness in a place where nothing is supposed to grow. Or is it more like one of those wonderful, local French red wines, the ones that you quaff rather than drink, the non-processed ones that unselfconsciously allow you to taste the very flavour and quality of the land that has produced them? Or is it deeper than that? Is it a function of harmony itself, a sense that when voices blend and resonate like this, it is possible to know for sure that sorrow and joy, the bass notes and the high ones, really do belong together in this life, and will be entangled and enmeshed in our experiences and our strivings until the very end has come? I don't know. I give up. I just love it.

4. Home Visits

B: Phyllis Chintu plonks herself down squarely on the wooden chair provided for her and smiles broadly at us. Her eyes are completely hidden by dark, silver-framed glasses, but I suspect they are twinkling. She exudes a comfortable efficiency. The warmth of her voice and the humour of her expression is an attractive combination. She stretches sturdy legs out in front of her and waves her feet at us.

"World Vision gives us our shoes. We walk miles in our job. It is exactly what we need most. Well," she pauses with an earthy chuckle, "that and our medicines of course!"

She turns her head to listen to a tiny woman sitting in the shade nearby who has whispered something in Bemba.

"Oh yes, as Mankina reminds me, our bags as well. Let's face it, the people at World Vision just like to keep us working!"

She includes Thom in her encompassing smile, places her hands firmly on her spread knees and raises an eyebrow expectantly.

"Now, what do you want to know?"

"Whatever you want to tell us. Or at least whatever you feel you've got time to tell us."

"Oh, we have a little time. It is important for you to understand. You see, when the virus first began to make people very, very sick no one knew what it was. Many had TB. Those who were ill were sent to the hospital. But there were so many, and the hospital asked for money, 7,000 kwacha for an X-ray alone. Sometimes we still have to take people to hospital if they are very sick, but many of our nurses have left Zambia for other places where they can afford to pay them more. There are only two nurses to 70 patients. Then if they have no money the doctor will not come and see the patient. The doctors give them vitamins and leave them to die. It is not a good system."

We never died like this before

"The health centres were not able to help much either. There were too many sick. Patients were seen faster and faster. There was no time to care for their needs. So then Sister Joanna, a Catholic nun, began the home-based care work. At first there were just Catholic volunteers, but now we come from all denominations. Our churches choose volunteers to go for training. Now we have 58 carers and 13 more are to be trained soon. It is something we can do. Well, all of us have seen friends suffer. Most of us have someone in our family who has died. So we have a heart for them.

"So that is why we try now, you know, to look after them in their homes. Now we have a better system of care in our community. We can take time. Listen to their needs. Our volunteers go each day in the morning and evening. At first, you know, we are not always welcome. We often find that all they want to do is rest in peace. But we try to teach them that it is possible to live with AIDS. We bring our clients strong antibiotics and make sure they take their medicine. The diocese also provides high-energy supplements which can make them feel a bit better. We take salt and mix it with water to bathe wounds. We give medicine to soothe coughs. We sweep the floor and bathe the children. We do whatever is necessary.

"And" (again a twinkle in Thom's direction), "when our shoes let in water or we run out of equipment, we turn to our partners for assistance."

"How do you know if there is an emergency?"

"Oh." Phyllis turns to the elderly lady again, this time with a sweet smile. "How do we know, Mankina?" She translates the question and we see Mankina shyly drop her eyes to the floor while the other carers sitting nearby laugh gently and nod in her direction.

"Mankina has been with the team from the very beginning. She is now in her seventies. You might think she would be feeling too tired to continue. But no. It is Mankina who goes early to all the houses we are at present visiting. At 5:30 in the morning. She makes her report and, when we arrive, she tells us who we need to visit urgently. She also tells us who has passed away in the night. That is very depressing, you know. Every day there is some heartbreak in Zamtan."

"But the new drugs? The anti-retrovirals. Aren't they helping?"

"Ah well, we do not have those drugs here. You must understand that AIDS is very tricky. It attacks each person in a different way, so you know there is not just one tablet that a sick person has to take to make them well. Each person has to have their own individual cocktail of drugs. And they have to take these drugs every single day for the rest of their lives. If they miss or they take the wrong dose they can make the disease worse. There are sometimes serious side effects like nausea and diarrhoea. So then they need to be given the drugs by someone with training in administering medicines. You have seen our roads here. How long it takes us to visit each of our clients. There are no telephones. No, it is not easy.

"Then there is the cost of the drugs. They are cheaper than they used to be, but did you know that even now they are subsidized they will still cost £5 every month? Most people here, even when they are well, only earn maybe £10 a month. How can they afford such things? Especially when they get sick and cannot work at all? So you see why we do not even bother to test the children to see if they are positive. Even if they are we cannot treat them at present. I have to say that for me the new drugs are not the whole answer to our problems. Maybe one day, but not yet."

"Phyllis, can we ask you something else? It's not exactly connected with what you do, but I have a feeling you'll know the answer better than most. Yesterday we went to the school AIDS club drama and choir presentations. We saw kids singing out loud songs about AIDS, about what to do and what not to do. About what AIDS is and what it does. It seems as though things are really forging ahead. But what do you think?"

We look at Phyllis and agree that here is a lady who is likely to know. Sitting there so serenely in her traditional paisley cotton *bubu* with short puffed sleeves, tight bodice and a scalloped neck, she gives the impression of being very much in charge. The distinctive uniform of the Home Care Team is bright green cloth, printed with pictures of a carer visiting a traditional Zambian home, and decorated with the universal symbol of AIDS, the red ribbon. Supplied by the diocese of Ndola, this material is made into various items of clothing so that members of the team are instantly identifiable and reassuring to the people they visit. Most of the team wear white blouses and uniform skirts. Mankina has a dress and hat fashioned out of the material. Phyllis merely ties a length of the material casually around her waist, thus retaining an air of separateness. A feeling that she is more than her uniform.

She is taking her time answering Adrian's question, and when she does her voice is slow and deliberate.

"I feel that it is moving forward in what they are doing, but the young ones are not really yet putting into practice what they are saying. By my own observations in the community I think that. Even with the schoolboys and schoolgirls, you know they sing about abstinence, but I don't think they are all listening to the message. Because if you come here in the evening you find children patronizing the bars, misbehaving. Sometimes they are very young. Ten, eleven, fifteen, you will find them. And I just wonder why they go, because poverty continues and I am sure the men abuse them for nothing. If they do give them money it will be very little, of that I am sure.

"I do not know why they are ignoring the message. I should say it is the fulfilment of the prophecy. The Bible says that in the end days children will not have respect for their parents. Will not fear their elders."

It is a very gloomy prognosis and Thom is looking a bit downcast. However, Adrian can't resist pointing out that Phyllis has already told him that she has five children, all of whom have apparently done very well and none of whom are 'misbehaving'.

"So," he says, "some young people must be taking notice."

Phyllis laughs her throaty laugh aloud.

"Ah, but I have taken it very seriously. I tell my children, and I tell my in-laws, too – the men my daughters have married. I am not afraid to tell them what I am thinking. We must not be afraid to speak. I think it is in families that we must speak. The schools do good work, but my children should respect me more than a teacher because I am a parent. And we do make steps forward. Not long ago we would not talk about sex."

An emphatic shake of the head emphasizes her point.

"Not at all. Not in families. It was a real taboo. Now we are all seeing death. A mother leaves five children for the grandmother to look after. We know we must speak. So the Home Care Team runs seminars here for mothers and couples and families."

'Here' is the circular stone bench on which we are sitting.

"We are seeing progress. We can talk about family planning. About staying safe. We can talk, too, about the facts of AIDS so people can help care for those in their families who are very sick. We teach the children how to do things to help their parents who are ill. And we tell them that you cannot catch it from sharing a drinking mug. Or sharing clothing. If sick folk are neglected they become depressed and their lifespan is shortened. We are seeing fewer stigmas and more hope coming into our lives as we learn how to live with AIDS in our community. Families are eating together again. Sick people are living longer. And, you know, we are fighting in a big battle but I do truly think that one day we will see the numbers come down."

"So it's not all bad news?"

"Oh no, at the moment the numbers are going up because many of us are infected, but one day. God willing. And meanwhile we will continue working – as long as people support us. We cannot continue if we do not have medicines and trained volunteers. So go back to your country and tell them in your homes."

A playfully stern wag of the finger accompanies her command.

"You have taken our nurses. You give us money for our medicines."

"Oh, we will Phyllis, we will tell them."

When it rains we stand in the corner

B: "When I die, who will look after my children? How will they survive? Because they are too small to do anything for activity. So how will they manage?"

Her energy spent from the longest sentence she has uttered since our arrival, Idah leans back wearily against a tree and gathers her cloak around her. She turns her head a little to focus on three of her children playing nearby as she continues in a rasping whisper. "They will need assistance.

Especially in the rainy season. You can see we need a new roof. When it rains we stand in the corner."

Hopelessness appears to seep through her bones and she settles into a strange faraway silence, her eyes no longer focused on this time and place. I watch her openly, knowing that she is no longer with us. I recognize this temporary disappearing as I have seen it all too recently, sitting as I did for hours next to my own mother as she gradually faded from this world, her life's energy consumed by the cancer which was to kill her. There is something else that is very similar, but I can't quite place it yet.

I continue to watch her. She lifts a corner of the cloth to wipe gathering beads of perspiration from her upper lip, and I am struck by her exquisite beauty and unconscious grace. Wide apart eyes, huge in her delicate face, the skin drawn taut over accentuated cheekbones. Idah Nkulaba could have graced our glossy magazine covers with her faun-like beauty.

Once I read an article about the clothes designer Roland Mouret, in which he recorded his insistence that all of the women who model his clothes should have size six hips, no more than thirty inches at their widest point.

Better come out to Zambia, then, is my bitter reaction. Never mind the sick hunt for anorexic products of our image-driven Western world. There are lots of size six women in Zambia, their bodies emaciated by a combination of poverty and whichever opportunist disease is sapping their life's energy. Come and meet Idah, for instance. Widow. Dying. Aged thirty-eight. Mother of five children, three under the age of eleven. The youngest, a small smiling girl with strands escaping from her tightly plaited hair, climbs onto her mother's lap and tucks herself confidently into the curve of her mother's arm.

Idah stirs, swivelling her head slowly, first in her child's direction and then in ours, apparently unsurprised that we are still here. She reaches out and teases one of the criss-crossing tiny plaits into shape.

"This is Mercy."

"What a beautiful name."

"When I was pregnant I was going through hardships and suffering, so when my daughter was born I called her Mercy."

"I am in Grade One. This is my doll."

Mercy puffs out her bony chest to show her 'doll' tucked into her sash. Made from a small stick with maize-bag string hair, this doll is clearly a very special friend.

I hear a cough behind me. Two boys have joined us. One of them, although quite sturdy, has a definite wheeze. They have come to introduce themselves, displaying the natural courtesy that is evident in so many Zambian children.

"I am in Grade One too. I like English and Maths."

"And you are …?"

"Stephen. This is my brother Golden (dragging the other boy forward) and then there are Kenedy and Collins."

Golden is grinning and holds out what is clearly his most prized possession for us to admire. It is round-ish, made of squashed plastic bags covered with the remains of a maize bag and tied firmly with string. It is, of course, his football. Maize bags have a thousand uses here in Zamtan.

Idah speaks again.

"They are good boys. They know I am ill. They help me with the wheelbarrow to collect the charcoal. They collect water. Kenedy is not here. He works. He is sixteen. He makes bricks. He earns 3,000 kwacha a week."

The children are bored. They have used up their being good. Golden throws his ball in the air and within minutes all three have vanished and, with them, their laughter, arguments and noise. Now the silence is harder to bear.

Thom, who has as usual been quietly assisting us with translation, leans forward.

"Idah, would you like to tell Adrian and Bridget what has happened to you?"

"I began to be ill six years ago." There is no animation in her voice. "My body was very weak. Then I began to have diarrhoea and a cough. Then my legs swelled. I was not in good health. Then my husband died."

After a considerable pause, the whispering monotone continues.

"My health was still not good. The Home Care Team came as usual to help me. They washed my clothes and brought me medicine. Sometimes food, haricot beans and soya. They told me I needed to give them some blood so they could test it. They tested it and found I was HIV-positive. I didn't believe it. I went to my church. I prayed."

"What did you pray, Idah?"

I looked in amazement at Adrian as he leaned forward to ask the question, his voice gentle with concern. I have to confess to you that my first thought was:

"You idiot! Why interrupt her in full flow with such a stupid question? It's obvious what she prayed for. Surely any fool would know she'd pray to be healed. I mean, how ..."

"I prayed, 'If it is your will, Lord, then let it be.'"

Just like that.

Suddenly I could put my finger on the similarity between thirty-eight-year-old Idah from Zamtan, Zambia, and eighty-eight-year-old Kathleen from Norwich, England. Through the rapidly thinning clay shells of their bodies and the accompanying frustration of helplessness, the light of faith could be seen shining. One day soon the clay will crumble to dust, but death will have no more victory over Idah than it had over my mother. There is no need to worry about her future. Any woman who, in spirit, could join Jesus in the garden of Gethsemane and accept the will of her father with such unswerving strength is safe indeed.

Which just leaves five children.

And the worry.

We all worry about our children, don't we? Who is picking them up from school? Will the babysitter look after them properly? We agonize over whether they are sleeping okay, eating okay, making friends at school okay. The list of our worries is never-ending.

Some of us, wherever we live in the world, have to worry about far worse scenarios than that. Because we are dying.

But, however terrible our situation, not one of us in the developed world can really identify with Idah. There are going to be five of them living on Kenedy's wages of less than £1 a week. One of them, Stephen with the nasty persistent cough, is almost definitely going to get very sick in the future. His caregiver is pretty sure that he is HIV-positive. Then there is Mercy. What is going to save her from one day deciding that her most valuable commodity is her body? Overnight, the mischievous, football-playing schoolboy Golden will become a mini-adult. We simply don't have a clue what it must feel like to sit weakly under a tree and worry about just how your beloved children are going to actually stay alive.

Food security

The phrase 'scrape something together for supper' takes on a whole new meaning when you live in an area like Zamtan. Even when I was the classic poverty-stricken student, that phrase meant we would scour the fridge, plunder the freezer, examine the tins in the cupboard, throw together something in the frying pan, make an omelette with leftovers. Leftovers! The luxury of having produced more than you can eat. For the majority of the inhabitants of Zamtan there isn't a lot to find to eat at all, and it requires a great deal of ingenuity, time and energy to get together even one small meal that has any nourishing content. There are certainly no foodstuffs that have gone past their sell-by date! No mouldy remains at the back of the fridge. No stale cereals or loaves of bread. In fact there is no rubbish whatsoever in Zamtan. No landfill sites. No need for education in recycling. Every single thing is used and reused.

'Food security' is a phrase we heard every single day during our visit to Zamtan. That means, quite simply, waking up every day of your life wondering not 'What will I eat today?" but "Will I eat today?" With 'food security' you will, quite literally, know where the next meal is coming from.

Zambia is, admittedly, a country of contrasts. In Kitwe, the nearest town, there is a very nice supermarket and even in Zamtan there is a shop run by no less than Rodrick himself. It has things on shelves. Not a lot, but certainly commodities such as loaves of bread, bottles of oil, jars of jam and cartons of long-life milk grace his shelves. He even has shampoo and headache tablets and, yes, you've guessed it... Coca-Cola! Yet even these basics would have been luxuries way beyond the means of most of the families we met.

No, thin *nshima* for breakfast and thicker *nshima* for supper is on offer in most households day after day after day. It's not too bad if it's flavoured with something. Otherwise it amounts to a swollen, tasteless lump of corn flour stodge that will at least fill your stomach for a while. There is nourishment in cereal but, whether turned into bread or boiled in water like rice and maize, it is, or should form, only part of a balanced diet. And the regular provision of even that basic staple is going to be a challenge for a family of orphans, four of whom are school age.

To cook *nshima* you need to buy ground maize. Or you can grow the sweetcorn yourself and dry it on your roof, in which case you will also need the means to grind it into flour. You then have to mix the flour with water, which you have to first collect from the pump or well, which could be some distance from your home. Then you need to make a fire. Gather wood or buy charcoal and matches. To prevent the spread of the tell-tale dry patches on the skin which indicate a poor diet, it is essential that you add protein. This will mean buying or catching *kapenta* (miniscule fish like whitebait), which populate the rare streams, or buying or catching rats that scurry through scrubby maize fields surrounding the village. There are no other sources of protein. No milk-producing cows grazing in green fields. No birds. Just imagine that – no birds.

Where have all the birdies gone?

A: Speaking of birds, I was really hoping to see some exotic specimens in Zambia. As a child I spent hours peering through the drawn curtains of our dining room window, hoping against hope that golden orioles and crossbills and Dartford warblers would grace our humble, crumb-strewn lawn with their rare presence so that I could mark them off as 'seen' in my *Observer's Book of Birds*. They never did, but I was quite happy to settle for the usual selection of sparrows, finches, thrushes and blackbirds, with occasional celebrity guest appearances by over-confident jays and even, on one exciting occasion, a green woodpecker. As an adult I am still interested in birds, even if I am not particularly well informed on the subject, and I was looking forward to seeing some of those interesting, brightly-coloured birds in Africa that I had only ever seen on television or on stamps.

Armed with a list of their names and a couple of sheets of illustrations I kept my eye open for the whole trip. I was willing just a few of them to appear. Apart from anything else some of the names were simply wonderful. I so wanted to catch sight of at least one or two species.

But where were they all?

I pined for the pallid honeyguide. I yearned for the yellow-billed oxpecker. I longed for the lazy cisticola. I desired the double-banded sandgrouse. I had a fundamental need for the knobbed coot. I craved contact with the collared palm-thrush. I wept for the woolly-necked stork. I raged for the red-headed weaver. I prayed for a peep at the purple-banded sunbird. In the end I would have settled for even a momentary glimpse of the green-backed camaroptera.

All to no avail. Zamtan in particular was an ornithological desert. In all the time that we were there I think I might have glimpsed one very small, dismally undistinguished, dull brown bird who looked very troubled, as if he might have lost his way and got separated from all the other very small dull brown birds.

It has been said, rightly in my view, that such things as friendship, art and philosophy are not essential to survival, but that they make survival worthwhile. I suspect that exotic birds might be included somewhere in that little list, and I am sure they are still to be found somewhere in Zambia. I hope they survive. However, like most other living creatures in places like Zamtan, they have learned that, until things change fairly radically, they are likely to be more desired for the nourishing quality of their flesh than for their beauty. They have voted with their wings, and who can blame them.

Smidgeons and morsels

B: There are few wild animals either, besides rodents. They have all been eaten out of existence long ago. Woe betide any rabbit foolish enough to visit Zamtan. Much of the ground is barren, hard and unyielding, producing little in the way of vegetation, so the best source of vitamins is likely to be a few cabbage leaves, sweet potatoes or beans, if you can afford them. These will need to be cooked, so maybe you can grow groundnuts or soya nuts, crack them and crush them to make oil to fry your leaves. The only fruit we found is called African biscuit. It has a thick brown husk and sparse flesh which tastes of sour lemons, but even that must be hunted for.

So we are talking about smidgeons, morsels, scraps, 'garnish' as we heard it described more than once, of protein or vegetables. Less than we would feed a small cat in the West. (My own two feline bossy boots turn up their noses at any but their favourite cat food – which costs me almost as much per day as Kenedy earns in a week.) Where will three young children manage to find the money or the time to gather together even a slender stock of such ingredients, let alone buy them?

I have only just begun, of course. There will be clothes that need to be washed and mended and a roof to be repaired before you run out of dry corners to stand in.

And this is just one family of orphans. In 2003 there were about a thousand orphans in Zamtan alone, seven hundred thousand in Zambia. Fourteen million orphans in the world. The devastation caused by HIV / AIDS is not lessening. In fact, it is increasing all the time. In this year alone, six hundred thousand parents will die in Zambia, leaving nearly a million new orphans. The individual personalities of the Stephens and the Goldens and the Mercys merge into overwhelming and alienating statistics.

It is difficult for us to get our heads round the fact that these are not cases of not bothering or not having the energy to make provision for their future. As I look at my pictures of Mercy and Stephen and Golden I struggle with the fact that there is hardly anything that can be officially done to secure the futures of wonderful children like these in a country which is no longer in a position to provide for its poor.

Maybe Idah's children have a *goma* who is still alive, a grandmother who, instead of relaxing in her old age and being cared for by her active children, will pick up the reins of parenting again. Everywhere in Zamtan we met not only grandparents but aunts, uncles and neighbours who have opened their doors to bewildered, bereft, hungry children. Children who, in addition to the trauma of witnessing chronic illness and the painful deaths of their mums and dads, will now have to cope with the stigma of their parents having died of AIDS and the suspicion that they themselves may be HIV-positive.

Which of course they might be. These acts of kindness have also meant, and will continue to mean for many years to come, that the families who have so generously accepted more children under their roofs will have to make their meagre resources go even further. The scraps will become scrappier. A bag of maize which would have lasted a week will last three days. So the children in families into which orphans come will also suffer. There will be more school uniforms and school books to buy. More children to become ill and need expensive medicines. Many children will just become too hungry and run away to the streets, huddling at night into piles like litters of kittens to share their warmth. The girls may well become involved with prostitution by their mid-teens, the boys with crime.

It's not surprising that there are dying women everywhere sitting under trees, watching their beloved children play, and worrying themselves silly. They turn their heads away in quiet despair at their inability to make anything better.

It's not surprising that we sit here in the developed world frustrated by our helplessness. We turn our hearts and minds away from the problem because our inability to make anything better defeats us.

But are we right? Is Idah right?

Well, not according to Rodrick and Agnes and Femmy and David and Charity and all of the rest of the committee of villagers who are absolutely determined that Zamtan can become a mini-welfare state if they can just lay their hands on some money to enable it to happen. And not according to Thom and Fordson and the rest of their energizing World Vision team who are absolutely determined to lay their hands on that money.

So it comes down to us. Again!

Sixty pence a day

What has happened to make us so anally retentive about our loose change? I am going to be brutally honest. Since coming back from Zambia I have been approached by person after person determined to express their anxiety over whether, if they were to become sponsors, all of their money would actually reach the person who needs it. Because if not, then count them out, at least for the time being. To support their argument they might shake their heads and refer to some newspaper article from eight years ago, or mutter about corrupt governments and inefficient middlemen.

I do know how they feel. I have been there. It is a grown-up thing to do with my money – to make sure I am not being taken for a mug, to decide that sometime in the future I may commit myself to a worthwhile cause, but I will wait until someone can prove to me that my money will be properly spent. I have done my share of muttering.

And I am ashamed of myself.

We are talking about sixty pence a day, for goodness sake.

What do we do with our sixty pence after we have so wisely decided it cannot be entrusted to foreigners? It is not enough for a cup of coffee in a café, but I suppose we could buy a newspaper to read about the terrible problems of the developing world.

That's a bit cynical isn't it? A bit intrusive.

Let me paint you some pictures instead.

Out of the stormy sea

The first picture is from a book published in 1890 called *In Darkest England and the Way Out*. It was written by William Booth, who founded the Salvation Army in response to the desperate needs of the poorest ten per cent in Britain at that time who, ironically, he equated with 'slaves in darkest Africa'!

I saw a dark and stormy ocean. Over it black clouds hung heavily; through them every now and then vivid lightnings flashed and loud thunders rolled, while the winds moaned, and the waves rose and foamed and fretted and broke and rose to foam and fret and break again.

In that ocean I thought I saw myriads of poor human beings, plunging and floating, shouting and shrieking, cursing and struggling and drowning; and as they cursed and shrieked, they rose and shrieked again, and then sank to rise no more.

And out of this dark and angry ocean I saw a mighty rock that rose up with its summit towering high above the black clouds that overhung the stormy sea; and all around the base of this rock I saw a vast platform; and on this platform I saw with delight a number of the poor, struggling, drowning wretches continually climbing out of the angry ocean; and I saw that a number of those who were already safe on the platform were helping the poor creatures still in the angry waters to reach the same place of safety. ...

And as I looked I saw that the occupants of that platform were quite a mixed company. That is, they were divided into different 'sets' or castes and occupied themselves with different pleasures and employments; but only a few of them seemed to make it their business to get people out of the sea. ... Some of them were absorbed day and night in trading in order to make a gain, storing up their savings in boxes, strong rooms and the like ... Many spent their time in amusing themselves with growing flowers on the side of the rock; others in painting pieces of cloth, or in playing music, or in dressing themselves up in different styles and walking about to be admired.

Some occupied themselves chiefly with eating and drinking, others were greatly taken up with arguing about the poor drowning creatures in the sea and as to what would become of them in the future, while many contented themselves that they did their duty to the perishing creatures by the performance of curious religious ceremonies. …

And all this time the struggling shrieking multitudes were floating about in the dark sea, quite nearby – so near that they could easily be rescued.

Trenches and pipes

The second picture is an experience Adrian had while sitting in church – a memory he recorded in *Growing Up Pains*.

A picture started to form in my mind of a huge lake surrounded by plots of land, each one occupied by a single person. Behind the plots that gave access to the lake were more plots, again occupied by individual people. As I explored the picture mentally, I saw that the lakeside dwellers were made up of two kinds of people. The first kind rushed to and fro from the edge of the lake to the boundary between their own plot and the one behind, carrying cups of water to their landlocked neighbours. Most of the water got spilled in the process, but they worked on frantically, doing their best. The other kind were not working frantically at all. They were simply digging steadily on their plots of land, with no apparent interest in the fate of the waterless tenants whose land adjoined theirs. One of the cup-carriers stopped, red-faced and breathless, and spoke with some annoyance to one of the diggers.

"Why don't you do as we do? Why don't you get a cup and carry water to those who have none? It is selfish to work only on your own land as you do."

The digger leaned on his spade for a moment and smiled. "You don't understand," he said, "I'm digging a trench."[1]

The situation. The problem. The ideal solution. Sorted.

"But," I hear you say, "it's not as simple as that. Oh yes, I get the point. Churches must stop navel gazing. Aid agencies can take a bow. But it doesn't work. Our neighbours in Zambia and countries like Zambia are not shrieking and drowning so close by that we can reach out and help them. If they were we would. Our neighbours in Zambia and countries like Zambia are not landlocked immediately behind us. If they were we could build such a trench and give them access to every drop of water they need. But they aren't and we can't. There are too many shrieking, dying souls. The numbers of drowning are increasing all the time. It is too late. We can't rescue them. They are too far away. Any solution we come up with will be imperfect. There will be waste. The aid will not get through completely. Let's wait until ..."

And I for the first time in my life want to get on a huge soapbox (whatever one of those actually is) and shout:

"Get real! Of course it's an imperfect solution. But it's the best we've got."

Let's take the image of the trench even further. Assume it is too simplistic. Decide that to get the water to other continents we would have to lay a pipeline. There will be initial costs to be met. Then, because we are inexperienced, those pipes will inevitably spring leaks. Water will be wasted. But, if we have overseers totally committed to improving the system, then the expertise in designing and laying pipes will be improving all the

---

[1] *The Growing Up Pains of Adrian Plass* (London: Marshall Pickering, 1986), pp. 144–45.

time. Expert engineers will be called in to strengthen the pipeline. Gradually less and less water will trickle away and more and more will reach the areas that need it. Mind you, it would be unrealistic to assume that we could relay such a system to everyone's door. It would cost a fortune. So at some point we would still need to employ people to transport tanks of water to the local villages. From there, willing volunteers will fill buckets and take them from door to door, allowing the desperately thirsty to cup their hands and drink. Strictly speaking, the doubters would be right. The thirsty won't get every drop originally intended for them, but they will get a darned sight more than they would if no one had bothered to send any.

Crystal rivers

I want to finish with a third picture. It is from Revelation, chapter twenty-two, verses one to three.

> The angel showed me a river that was crystal clear, and its waters gave life. The river came from the throne where God and the Lamb were seated. Then it flowed down the middle of the city's main street. On each side of the river are trees that grow a different kind of fruit each month of the year. The fruit gives life, and the leaves are used as medicine to heal the nations. (CEV)

Only then, when God has created a new heaven and a new earth, will there be a perfect solution. Idah will soon be dipping her toes in the crystal rivers, but down here her children remain, and there will be only be imperfect solutions offered by imperfect old us. But they can get better. They are getting better. The morning after Adrian and I met Idah we witnessed one way in which this is happening.

5. Self-sufficiency

B: Each time we entered Zamtan along the wide dirt track that leads to the half-built community centre we passed a little house that, in contrast to the bleakness of its neighbours, looked like a fairy-tale cottage. Bougainvillea covered the small gate porch and we caught glimpses of happy children playing in the shade of trees, and there were real flowers and neat rows of maize growing in dark moist soil. There was even what looked like a well. To quote a popular UK quiz show that we sometimes found ourselves watching: 'Who lives in a house like this?'

This morning we were to find out.

"Pigs," Rodrick had announced emphatically in our early morning meeting, as yet again he took time out from running his shop to fill us in on what we were going to be shown that day, "are definitely best."

We had learnt to stay quiet during these meetings, knowing that eventually we would understand statements as intriguing as this one.

"Oh, yes. You have seen how many extra mouths many, many of our people have to feed. We on the committee responsible for orphans and vulnerable children have had to ask ourselves this question. 'How can they do this when they cannot make enough money to even feed their own family?' So then we are looking all the time for new ways for these families to generate an income. World Vision has very much experience in this and they have given us whatever we needed to start a new enterprise. All are good but pigs are best, as you will see today ..."

Thom takes up the thread after we have waved goodbye to Rodrick so that he can return to help his lovely wife, who has been left holding the fort.

"We try constantly to encourage new enterprises which help families to be independent. Of course, not everyone here can work. Many of the orphans are too small and too weak and we have a large number of sick folk who cannot use their hands. So then we try and help in other ways. We can give grants, food assistance. You have seen that. But for the great numbers who want to work but cannot find work, especially the women who are looking after our orphans, the aim is to give them self-generating incomes. Our part in it is to support the community's initiatives. So we might give wool to the women to begin crocheting so they can then sell what they have made, buy more wool and still have a little money over. Or present a family with some chickens. Now, chickens are good because they do not need much looking after, and of course they provide the protein in the eggs and also chicks to share with other families. Then we have chosen five families who are looking after orphans and sent the teenagers and adults for courses in tailoring, carpentry or batik and tie-dye. We provide sewing machines to some other women so they can sew dresses, and especially school uniforms. We are helping them to make bricks as you will see later today.

"We used to be involved with micro-enterprise in a bigger way, but it is very time-consuming and we do not have what I think you call a nose for business. So Fordson has linked us up with a company called Hammas, another Christian organization, who help our people to properly market what they have produced. It is all going very well and we are looking, as Rodrick said, for new ways. Farmer Cedric has promised to give the village some land to use for agriculture and they are beginning fish farming in some of our big ponds. *Kapenta*, you understand, not large fish. Again, we are providing what they need to get going – after that it will be up to them. Rodrick tells me they are also considering goats, but of course there are drawbacks."

"Oh, but I thought that goats were easy. After all they eat anything, don't they?"

"Precisely!"

"I'm sorry, I don't understand."

"They might eat the little crops that the poor families do manage to grow. After all, what else is there for goats to graze on?"

Point taken.

"But pigs, in our opinion, are, as Rodrick says, the best. There are five piggeries in our community now. We have supplied the first litters and of course enough mash to feed the first generation. People living here do not have many nourishing scraps to give them! Then when the sow has piglets we will take some and distribute them among the community so that more piggeries will come into being. One sow will be kept for giving birth to more piglets. The rest the owner can nurture for a few months until they are big enough to sell. A pig will fetch 7,000 kwacha a kilo live, and 9,000 kwacha slaughtered. With the income generated more mash can be bought ready for the next litter. The rest can be used for day-to-day living."

So a grown pig could make between £25 and £60. Even we could see that this is real money!

"Mind you," continued Thom, "we choose who we give pigs to very carefully. They need a lot of looking after. We had no hesitation in giving one of our piggeries to David and Elizabeth Daka. They have been helping us for ten years in the community and have taken in no fewer than nine orphans. To give them this means of support is our way of saying 'thank you' for everything they have done."

We knew David. A soft-spoken, grey-haired man who appeared to be very much Rodrick's right-hand man. One of the tireless caregivers, he had an aura of modest competence. But who was Elizabeth?

The owner of the fairy cottage, no less! She emerges smiling from her front door as soon as we reach her gate. No doubt one of her many children had been on lookout duty and run to tell her that we were on our way. We would not have noticed. We had become accustomed to acting like Sellotape to the throng of small people playing at the side of the track, arriving at our destinations with a cluster of chattering children attached.

As soon as I see her I know I had it right. Everything about her is pure story book. Her smile, her funny bonnet with its string decoration, her bright pretty dress which hangs loosely on her little frame, the laughter lines around her huge deep-set eyes, and above all a sense that she loves life. All emanating from this woman like a wonderful perfume.

"Welcome, welcome!"

"Elizabeth, we have come to see your pigs."

With a small bob curtsey she indicates the entrance of the pig house with an outstretched arm. Then she proudly leads the way, carefully undoing the string fastening on the door and ushering us all in. It is dark inside, the only light coming from the tiny triangular windows cut into the concrete walls. But there is sufficient light to see that this is a decidedly des res for pigs. It is dry, clean, roomy and snug.

"I can't help feeling," whispers Adrian, "that Lackson and Philemon would be more than happy to move in here! No holes in this roof."

A huge porcine sigh leads us to the sow. She is enormous. Standing squarely, her face lifted in anticipation of a stroke, or more likely her next meal of mash, she completely fills her pen. Strident squeals lead us to the next pen, where there are at least ten piglets tumbling over each other in excitement. Elizabeth leans over and, with a showman-like flourish, opens the door between the pens. There is a rush of miniscule legs and snouts, a thud as their mum hits the floor, a rising tide of squeals as the piglets fight over the best teat and then a snuffling quiet as they settle down to feed. The sow looks up at us with a decidedly smug expression on her face and then sighs again as if to say, "A woman's work is never done." It makes us all laugh, including Elizabeth, who is clearly enjoying every moment.

"Trust a proud mother never to miss a photo opportunity," mutters Jim, as he leaps into action with his camera.

"She's a real ham," adds Adrian (who never has let the unfunny nature of his comments stop him from making them).

We stand and gaze to our heart's content, drinking it all in. At last a sign of something approaching prosperity. Of hope. Of food security. We look at the children crowding the doorway. I catch the eye of one of them, a sturdy little girl with enormous saucer-like eyes, and she gives me a dazzling ear-to-ear smile. I look across at Adrian.

He whispers, "And if each time there's a litter a new piggery gets set up, think what it'll mean."

I look at the piglets, their tiny tummies visibly swelling with milk. I look back at the children in the doorway.

"Full bellies all round," I whisper back as we turn to leave this scene of utter contentment and re-enter the starker world outside.

Penelope, the most important person in the world

A: I noticed the little girl with the enormous saucer-like eyes as well, and a familiar thought occurred to me.

Before telling you what it was I ought to explain that my family and friends are more or less accustomed to hearing me say slightly peculiar things. Perhaps they have finally accepted that there is a level of strangeness above which I am never likely to rise, and below which I am incapable of falling. Those who know me less well are occasionally a little puzzled by my comments. Recently, for instance, I was in a car with someone I know only slightly. We stopped at a pedestrian crossing to allow a tall, thin, rather unhappy looking woman to pass from one side of the road to the other.

"Look," I murmured, "there goes the most important person in the world."

"Do you know her?" enquired the man next to me, perfectly reasonably.

"Oh, no," I replied, "I've never seen her before."

I had to explain to my bemused companion that, ever since becoming a Christian, I have been overwhelmed by the paradoxical, unarguable fact that, in some way I will never understand on this side of the grave, every individual in the entire world is the single most important person in the eyes and heart of God.

Exactly those same words passed through my mind when I first met little Penelope in the yard of Elizabeth's house. I don't quite know why. They just did. She was a small, round-faced person with a snub nose and the kind of built-in smile that cannot fail to build up your faith in the power of good things. Like so many other children in Zamtan she had lost her mummy and her daddy to the senseless ravages of HIV/AIDS, but she had then had the good fortune to be adopted by Elizabeth and her husband David.

We didn't have much of a conversation, Penelope and I, but we did lean side by side against the angle of the wall like old friends, and we exchanged smiles.

When Bridget and I got back to England and were looking through all the photographs that had been taken during our trip, we realized to our surprise that, although we hadn't noticed it at the time, little Penelope, with that semi-circular, child's drawing of an engaging grin always in place, had been quite close to us in all sorts of situations. She popped up in lots of different places, sometimes at the back of a crowd, and sometimes in the foreground, rather like the child in the red coat in *Schindler's List*.

All over Zamtan. All over Zambia. All over Africa. All over the world. They pop up everywhere. Little children who need to be rescued by assistance or sponsorship from the bad, bad place where life has thrown them. Little children like Penelope. Look at her face. Look at their faces. Whatever you do, don't underestimate their value in the eyes of God. They are the most important people in the world.

The other side of the wall

A: "Oh, no! I'm so sorry. I didn't realize that they would be that soft and...oh, dear, I am so very sorry."

As I stared in disbelief at the dent I had made in one of the Zamtan community's precious building blocks, I wished I could be anywhere else. I could feel waves of disapproval washing over my miserable, guilt-infested being. They emanated from just behind my right shoulder. My wife was not impressed, to say the least. Those who had been toiling away to make the bricks just smiled and gestured with careless waves of their hands that it didn't matter. I shouldn't worry. Nice, but it only made me feel worse.

It was inevitable that this incident should remind me of my long and dismally undistinguished record in the field of poking and pulling at things until they break or crack or are damaged in some other way. It is a shameful catalogue of events. Come away from Zambia with me for a moment or two to the fair land of Scotland and I will tell you all about the most memorable example, for me at any rate, of this unfortunate habit.

Once upon a time, only a year or so before our trip to Africa, in fact, Bridget and I were in the middle of a short bed and breakfast vacation in the west of Scotland. At a local shop in the coastal village where we spent the first night of our holiday we happened upon – and by some miracle agreed to buy – a not very expensive but exquisitely wrought piece of pottery with a smooth, glass-like base of the deepest, purest dark blue. We were fascinated by the pleasingly irregular shape and the shell-like delicacy of our new acquisition. The lady who owned the shop told us that this and similar pieces were supplied to her by a potter who lived and worked in a remote hillside location several miles inland to the north. Bridget and I looked at each other with a mutual surmise. We were on holiday and in holiday mode. Our next planned destination was no great distance from our present location, certainly not more than a loch and a half away. Time was the least of our problems. We decided to search out this pottery and see what else might be on offer. Apart from anything else there was a question in our minds about that stunningly rich, glassy-blue base. We were curious about what it was actually made of and how the artist had achieved such a striking effect. As we set off through the dripping morning air in our little hired car we hugged to ourselves a pleasant sense of anticipation. Small, unexpected adventures have a tingling cosiness all of their own.

We did find our pottery in the end, but only, honesty compels me to admit, after being seduced by a succession of vaguely worded signs that finally led, after mile upon mile of twisting, tiny lanes, to the wrong gallery – one that proudly exhibited some of the least inspiring paintings we had ever seen. Having actually arrived there it seemed churlish to turn and leave immediately. We gazed around at the myriad luridly coloured seascapes adorning the walls of what appeared to be a converted barn as the artist, a classic example of those immensely energetic, short balding men in their late fifties who wear shorts and open-toed sandals and have taken early retirement from teaching, explained that he prided himself on never taking more than 45 minutes to complete a painting. His pride was demonstrably not misplaced. The most cursory glance confirmed the fact that these were indeed pictures that could not have taken more than three quarters of an hour to paint. We muttered words of pallid insincerity about his courageous use of colour and his bold disdain for anything so trivial as detail, and left as soon as we decently could.

It took us another half-hour of twisting, climbing progress in our car to get to the place we had been looking for in the first place. If anything, it was even more remotely situated. Set on the side of a steep hill and lying at the end of a long grassy track, it consisted of a low, whitewashed single-storey cottage beside a spacious barn, possibly, we conjectured, the place where a kiln was likely to be located. It was a beautiful, solitary spot. Turning our car engine off, we sat with the doors open for a moment or two, in a silence broken only by the odd burst of birdsong and the wind soughing through the top branches of leggy trees that ringed an expanse of emerald green grass in front of the two buildings.

There seemed to be no one about and ours was the only car in sight. We plied the knocker on the front door, gently at first, and finally with the kind of vigour that you can only allow yourself when you are 90 per cent sure that nobody is in. All to no avail. We tried calling out, but no one appeared. A brief tour around the outside of the house and barn was equally unsuccessful. It was so frustrating. We knew we were in the right place. Cupping our hands against the glass of one of the cottage windows, we had been able to clearly see, arrayed on a wooden shelf, examples of the potter's art, one or two of them similar to the item we had bought earlier in the day. But how long would we have to wait before the owner returned? Suppose he was away for the night? Suppose he had gone to Luton for a week? Or Greenland for a fortnight?

"Let's have a look in the barn," said Bridget, "I think the doors are open."

She was right. And our instinct about the kiln was correct as well. As we entered through the big wooden doors we saw a big metal oven at one end of the barn. Beside it, on racks attached to the wall, rows of pale, handcrafted pots were waiting to be baked to that miraculous, brittle hardness that makes them beautiful and functional. One pot in particular caught my attention. It was tall and slender, a waisted vase or urn. It appeared, to my untutored eye, to be in the Grecian style. A finely wrought, curled handle had been fashioned out of a separate piece of clay and fastened to the upper side of the pot. The whole thing struck me as being a marvellously subtle piece of work.

There is absolutely no excuse for what I did next. I seem to recall D.H. Lawrence saying or implying something in his novel *Sons and Lovers* about women needing to pick flowers so that they can own the beauty of the blooms, while men are simply content to look at them. Which all goes to show that Lawrence said some very silly things as well as being a great writer. My wife would never have touched that pot. Something in me just had to. And that 'something' seemed to be beyond my control. Of course I cannot seriously claim that my hands operate independently of my will. That would be ridiculous. All I can say is that I watched with a sort of hypnotized horror as my left hand reached slowly out towards the handle of the pot, rather in the manner of those dumbly disobedient claw things in the glass cages that never win you anything at fairgrounds, until I was able to grasp the delicately sculpted handle between my finger and thumb and give it the tiniest of experimental tweaks.

Why? Why did I do it? What on earth or even in Scotland did I think was going to happen when I gripped a piece of unfired pot and gave it a twist? You would not have needed to be Nostradamus to predict the outcome of this foolish action. The entire handle came away in my hand, taking a significant section of the main body of the pot with it.

I froze. Then, presumably afflicted by some pathetically optimistic notion that time itself might be reversed, I moved my hand slowly back into the position it had occupied before the awful moment of separation. No miracle. The damage was permanent. A beautiful object had been destroyed. Still holding the sharp breath I had taken a few seconds ago, I placed the detached piece of pottery down on the shelf beside the vase and walked into the open air. Bridget, who had been distracted by a different shelf of pots and was unaware of my act of vandalism, followed me.

"What's the matter?" she asked, after overtaking me and studying my drawn face for a moment or two.

I expelled the breath and took another one before replying.

"I've broken a pot," I explained in brittle, conversational tones. "Looks like a very expensive one. Not much less than a hundred quid, I should think. Pulled the handle off. I didn't mean to do it. It just ..."

Without speaking she turned back into the barn, returning after a few seconds to perform the sighing, head-shaking, tongue-clicking ritual with which she is wont to greet fresh evidence of my disastrous inability to simply leave things alone. Then, after about half a minute, and at exactly the same moment, we turned and looked into each other's eyes. An unspoken but perfectly clear communication took place.

"Look," we were saying silently to each other, "the area around this house and barn is as hushed and deserted as it was when we first arrived. If we want to, we can walk over there, climb quietly into our car, start the engine and disappear. No one will ever know who was here or how the pot got broken. They might assume that the handle just fell off on its own somehow. Who knows? Maybe it was a faulty one anyway. Let's face it, we'd look pretty silly hanging around waiting for them to come back only to discover that the stupid vase was about to be chucked in the bin anyway. Yes, perhaps it would be best if we just went..."

It's a funny thing, but when we talk about facing a moral dilemma, we often do not actually mean that at all, do we? What we are really saying is that we face a choice between sacrificing what we want at the altar of what we believe, or simply taking what we want. In other words, the inner debate is not concerned with which of two courses is the more morally desirable. Rather, it is about whether the moral system by which we claim to live actually affects our choices when we are faced with a personal sacrifice, and particularly on those occasions when there will be no audience to judge or influence the decision we make. We are frail creatures.

Fortunately, between us Bridget and I just about stitch together to make up one whole Christian. We married for better or for worse, and we do try to make sure that our mutual support facilitates the former rather than the latter. Sometimes we fail. This time we survived. The area around those buildings was not deserted. Of course it wasn't. And if we had convinced ourselves that it was, nothing would have meant very much any more. We waited, and eventually the potter, a very friendly young lady as it turned out, returned home to find us sitting in our car, Bridget quietly reading, while I rehearsed ways of telling her that her beautiful work of art had been damaged.

She was very nice about it all, if a little surprised that we had remained on the scene of the crime. A little later, sitting in the house with cups of tea and coffee, we discovered that the precious vase would have retailed at £75. Learning that a repair was not possible we insisted that she take £50 to cover the time that it had taken her to actually make the object. She reluctantly accepted. We also bought a few more of the little pots with the blue bases. But how, we asked, did she manage to achieve that deep blue colour and such a smooth, glassy finish?

"Bristol Cream," was the artist's bright but enigmatic reply.

"Bristol Cream?" I repeated vacantly.

"Yes, you know, the sherry. It comes in those dark blue bottles. I smash the bottles up, melt the glass, and then use it for the bases of the pots."

"Aaah, of course! Bristol Cream. Of course ..."

I shall tell you why Scotland was so important in a moment.

Meanwhile, back to Zamtan and the brick-poking episode. I can see the scene in my mind's eye as if it were happening before me. The actual brick-making machine is quite new. At this stage in its existence rust is nothing but an unpleasant rumour. The device stands like some giant children's toy, a blue and red metal monster on wheels, the height of a man, with a rectangular container at the base and long handles stretching up at the top. This is the sort of thing that, in a childlike manner, you wish you could have one go at but would hate to spend the whole day toiling over. Those handles have to be pulled and pressed down in order to create a pattern of spaces in the completed bricks. Each time the handles are hauled down, three complete bricks will be made and left to dry in a row on a solid platform with the others, while the machine is wheeled back a few feet so that the process can be repeated.

A dozen or so members of the committee cluster around the machine. Slightly to our bewilderment, we register the fact that they are largely the same people who are involved in all of the other projects and activities that we have been invited to witness. People like the ubiquitous chairman, Rodrick Ngoma, and smartly dressed Charity Nambeye who is involved in all sorts of constructure activities. It feels a little like a television 'soap', one of those series set in some unfathomably strange village where no more than a handful of people ever actually appear in the local pub or the village shop or the doctor's surgery. I know the reason for it in this instance, though. It is because all of these folk really mean business in this community. They appear at every juncture because they are willing to do anything and everything. They are Zamtan residents wedded to many causes and, in this case, to the cause of raising money for orphans and vulnerable children. This valuable self-sustaining brick-making project, funded by World Vision (who bought the machine and supplied the first bags of cement), is helping the people to be self-sustaining. Some of the bricks will be sold for 2,800 kwacha (about 40 pence) each, while others will be used to repair old buildings or build new dwellings for those who need them. And there is no hierarchy here. No supervisors. No Little Red Hens. Everyone does the work and gets involved in the process, men and women working together, taking turns to mix piles of cement with shovels, fill the mould with the mixture and smooth it with special tools, drag the heavy handles down in order to shape the finished bricks, and finally heave the heavy machinery along its concrete base a sufficient distance so the whole cycle can start over again. Such energy. Such dedication. Mind you, it does remind us just a little of grown-ups making sandcastles – I suppose because they are all so keenly excited to demonstrate the project to us.

And as for me? Ah, as for me. What do I do? What is my contribution to all this bright, practical endeavour? Well, I have already shared the sad tale with you. My fantastic contribution is to take a few steps forward and allow that same dangerous hand to reach out and poke a hole in one of their carefully constructed sandcastles with my finger. Starkly incongruous visions of Scottish countryside flicker across my consciousness like picture postcards as I draw back in horror, a Pavlovian response triggered no doubt by the sighing, head-shaking, tongue-clicking sound effects that are proceeding from she who has honed these signals of disapproval to perfection.

It seems like a small thing, I suppose. It was only one brick, and in any case, as I have already said, the genial members of the committee just smiled and shook their heads and didn't seem to mind. But when I got back to the guest house that evening and was sitting drinking tea on the veranda as the African dusk swiftly descended, I found myself spiralling down into something of a mini-depression about the incident. Did it not amount to a symbol of this whole trip that we were making? Here we were in Zambia, a country we knew nothing about and had rarely given a thought to before World Vision suggested the trip. We were supposed to be investigating the lives of men and women who surely had enough problems without two overfed English people poking and prying into everything they did and were trying to do. Might we break or dislodge something without really meaning to? Was the whole endeavour really going to be worthwhile? Would our constant questions and our interminable jottings actually result in something that might help these gentle, courteous people in their battle against grinding poverty and the terrifying waves of sickness that were flooding their country?

Well, inadequate or not, we would try. We would certainly do our best.

"But how exactly," I asked God in my mind, "are we going to do it? How are we going to make a difference to the way people think in our part of the world? The need of the developing world is like a leech clinging to the skin of so many Christians in the West. Irritating. Blood-sucking. Worth wasting just enough salt on to make sure that it drops off and goes away for a while. I can't kid myself. I have been just the same in the past. What is the truth? Which is the right path for us to be taking? How should we Christians be thinking?"

Unexpectedly, Scotland comes back into my mind. The sort of moral dilemma that is not genuinely a moral dilemma at all. This time it is not about the choice between owning up to breaking a vase or scuttling away before the owner returns. This time it is about men, women and children, many of them our brothers and sisters in Jesus, whose need is like an open wound on the body of Christ. Do we help or do we not? As Bridget has already said, if they lived next door, or in the flat downstairs from us, or on the other side of the road, we would see and hear for ourselves that they have barely enough food to (literally) keep body and soul together, and that mortal illness is raging through them. I think many of us would do something. We would mobilize our church into helping. We would feed and visit and care and get involved. We would not be able to sleep in our beds as long as we knew that such suffering was being endured only yards from our door and that our response was to do nothing.

Are we going to let ourselves neglect these needy folk because of a convenient or inconvenient accident of geography, or are we going to be the hands and feet of Jesus in bringing aid and comfort to the people he loves, and thereby to him? That is our dilemma, or our choice. That is the question for all of us. God watches and waits for each one of us to answer it. Is our faith just a pleasantly organized game? Or is it for real? Does it make us do things? Does it?

Can I hear them weeping just over there on the other side of the wall? If the answer is that I can, am I going to do anything about it?

6. Sports for Life

B: "And now Mr Kennedy, who is known to us to be the first student from these parts to go to the university in Lusaka, is taking the ball round the defender. Oh, foul shot! Foul shot indeed!"

The Zamtan sound system is in use again. Yellow cap firmly in place, Rodrick and his megaphone are having the time of their lives. And so are we. Seated under an

 awning supported by lengths of wood, behind two bored-looking representatives from Zambian national television, we are watching the most exhilarating football match ever. Over the last three weeks, qualifying contests have been played in the three villages that come under

the World Vision umbrella of care, and now, at Sports for Life day, we are watching the grand final between Kakolo village and Lubuto.

"Foul shot! We want to see fair play. Sport is for living. Down with discrimination. We appeal to the referee, Mr Kwsowa, to see fair play. Very nice haircut, Mr Kwsowa. Very nice."

The unusual commentary, accompanied by loud heckling and shrieks of laughter from the ladies sitting on the benches behind Rodrick, has much in common with the one that accompanied the Dodo race in *Alice in Wonderland*. Indeed, if one did not know that the Sports for Life day had been specifically organized by World Vision and the committee as a means of both communicating the message about AIDS and promoting an alternative healthy lifestyle, one might be even more bemused. Looking round the jostling sea of supporters, I can see why Rodrick is able to deliver such a frivolous commentary. A deeply serious man, wholly committed to preventing AIDS from wiping out his beloved village, he and the committee he leads have understood that the creation of an army fit for fighting must begin with the re-creation of a sense of community.

Reversing the trend

The sheer weight and size of current problems – not just here, but throughout Africa – have been threatening to tear to shreds the close-knit groups of folk who once cared for each other above all else. There was a time when, if you had more maize than your neighbour, you shared it. If you had a roof over your head you extended a welcome to any who needed shelter, especially family. Kinship was crucial, a priority. Now, this deadly combination of hunger and HIV/AIDS has brought a new kind of fear that breeds a different set of priorities. For the first time in their history, families and individuals have begun to look out for number one.

Here in Zamtan there is a determination to reverse that negative trend. Actually, Rodrick Ngoma is himself a living symbol of that determination. A former army gunner, he spent two years in prison, wrongfully accused of treason. He is also the father of two children, one seriously disabled, and he has two orphans at home. Rodrick obviously feels the weight of injustice and poverty personally, but instead of reacting with bitterness he is now using his leadership skills to benefit the community. Things really are beginning to change for the better.

Turning to World Vision for help, the committee, under Rodrick's leadership, have drawn on that organization's experience to devise schemes that will help in building back confidence. This Sports for Life day is one of the suggestions that they have taken up. A tool for living positively under the shadow of AIDS. Sports for Life.

The training has been intense and, to give the tournaments the dignity they merit, World Vision has provided authentic kit for both the boys' football and the girls' netball teams.

Netball in Zambia, by the way, seems a rather more vivid and vigorous game than the matches I have seen in England. After the eventful and dramatic netball final, I had the opportunity to meet one of the captains, eighteen-year-old Gertrude Kambwali.

Oh, yes!

There was nothing remotely frivolous about the tall, handsome schoolgirl who stood in front of me. It quickly became clear that Gertrude had little need for Charity – team coach, committee member, and a person we were coming to regard as our friend – to interpret for her. Her English was excellent.

"It is very important to me to play netball and to be captain. Important to my community. We start to meet together and so it came about that those who were willing would join together to play sports like this. It is a way we see to keep us safe from HIV/AIDS. That is how we joined."

"We meet every week." She smacked a clenched fist repeatedly on the palm of her other hand to emphasize the importance of what she was saying. "Regularly. Every week. We meet to train and then there is this tournament. We met for the quarter-finals in February, and now this day you see us meet again for the final. We have been playing for one year now."

Delighted by our amazement at the short length of time it has taken the teams to reach their potential she bobbed modestly, a broad smile on her face, before continuing confidently. "World Vision gave us our uniforms. We appreciate it. They are very smart. We can play with pride in our appearance. And, you see, we all know that spending time here, all of us doing something together, being part of something all together, playing, we are forgetting about boys. We are abstaining from doing something sexual."

She nodded her neatly braided head vigorously, determined for us to follow what she was saying.

"It is making a difference. Oh yes. All the teaching, all the singing and learning in church and in school and here even at a football and netball match is education in the community and it is working. I know among my friends we are taking notice. Yes, very much we are taking notice. It is easier for girls to say 'no' to boys because boys too are hearing information and they understand more."

She paused for breath and looked sternly at her coach, Charity, who had dissolved into a paroxysm of embarrassed giggles at such outspokenness. It struck me that, when it comes to talking about sex, there is as much of a generation gap here as there is anywhere else in the world! The difference is that Charity is only about ten years older than Gertrude. A clear indication that the freedom to speak openly is extremely new.

"No – no, there is nothing funny. Why do you laugh?"

Charity tried to control herself, hand over her mouth, only her laughing, rolling eyes conveying her discomfiture.

"It is nature. We know this. It is serious that as girls we are able to say 'no'. That we are informed why we must do this. Because otherwise, if I did not know, I am ending up doing something sexual. Oh yes."

Her frown deepened and she shook her head slowly.

"And me – I am then digging my own grave. No, it is better to play netball."

So there it was. Safety in netball. Tournaments like these are the eye of the storm.

As I watched Gertrude run off to return to her friends, and presumably to relate robustly what she had just told us, I couldn't help feeling sorry for any uninformed Zamtan youths who tried it on with this particular netball team.

The whole community?

In front of the awning where commentator and judges are sitting, two rickety school desks have been set up. These precarious pieces of furniture are covered by a long coloured cloth, decorated and anchored by two potted plants, one at each end. It is on this cloth that the prizes and trophies, also supplied by World Vision, are neatly arrayed in preparation for the grand presentations that will be made at the end of the afternoon.

In one sense, the numbers that have turned up indicate that the venture has been successful. It looks as if the whole community has decided to be involved in some way. At intervals throughout the day there have been brisk marching displays by the well-drilled local Scout troop, armed with long thin white sticks. They chant and sing as they are led in military fashion around the field by a man whose badge of authority appears to be one bright red woollen glove worn on his right hand. The sound of drums from impromptu performances by various small bands adds to the atmosphere, and there have been strange tribal dances featuring a man with a white-painted face wearing – please let this be just a coincidence – a shirt featuring the face of Saddam Hussein. One might be forgiven for assuming that half the populace support the French football team, as boys and men everywhere are sporting bright blue football shirts with 'Thierry Henry' emblazoned on the back. We are just a little wiser than we were. We know about Gifts In Kind now. We know that a shipment of surplus, shiny football shirts will have been snapped up and worn with pride regardless of the team the wearer happens to support. The sea of matching blue shirts just adds to the carnival quality of the day.

"And now the manager, Mr Fordson Kafwetu, has the ball. He is giving it everything he has. Oh, a magnificent try on the goal by the World Vision manager! Oh, no, it is offside!"

Groans and drum-beating and whistling from Fordson's supporters

"And now the ball has been kicked into touch by Harbelo, trained in piggery two weeks ago. Very nice play, Mr Harbelo. Remember Abstinence. Fight

Rois

Angels on bicycles

Lackson and Philemon – ratcatchers extraordinaire

The girl in the pink frilly dress

Adrian, Femmy and a badly damaged roof

AIDS club drama

Joyce and her precious paper

Phyliss and the home-based care team

Idah, Golden, Stephen and Mercy

Golden and his maize bag football

Elizabeth and her piglets

Bridget and Elizabeth

Making bricks

Penelope – the most important person in the world

A striking contrast in footwear

Carnival without food

Discrimination. Throw in to Kakolo village. To be taken by Mr Kerries. Congratulations on the birth of your new grandchild, Mr Kerries – oh no, now, that is not how we do it!"

Boots

A nasty collision between three players has occurred, and one of the yellow team is writhing on the ground. Mr Kwsowa of the nice haircut is there. So, too, are the members of both teams and a good portion of the audience, who are then shooed back to the side by a wild looking, extremely drunk individual brandishing a stick. Everyone has a great deal of advice to offer the referee.

The problem, as I see it, is complicated by the players' varying footwear.

Now, having raised three sons, I know a great deal about football boots. I know about the aerodynamic ones that will enable you to bend it like Beckham, the ones that (apparently) everyone else has except you and cost the equivalent of a month's mortgage. I know about the difference between fixed studs and unfixed studs, which either become so embedded that you cannot remove them with the little tool they provide or detach themselves and get lost as soon as you put your foot on the ground. I know about the kind of boots that possess the power to totally disappear five minutes before you need to leave the house. And I also know everything there is to know about cleaning them!

Over the years I tried everything. There was the "You are all going to clean your own boots every week" phase, which resulted in the pipes that ran from the kitchen sink being clogged with foul-smelling mud and eventually needing a plumber. Then there was the "clean them outside" era, which resulted in slippery clods of grassy earth being left all over the back step. Forks used for wheedling the matted grass from between the studs look as though they had all been in the company of Uri Geller. One mother I was commiserating with recently said she had found a tomato pipper invaluable for the task. Having recommended it to several of her friends, she caused one particular door-to-door salesman to ponder deeply over the new-found popularity of this modest kitchen utensil. The worst phase of all was the one in which I decided to remove all pressure and let them be told off by their manager for turning up with filthy boots. I should mention to any mother wearily thinking she will follow suit that the smell of boots left to rot for a week in a carrier bag under a bed is unique and truly terrible.

What I had no experience of whatsoever was the cheaper, easier version of playing football that I was witnessing now – the one where you wear no boots at all. I could see that it would be no problem if you were playing against non-boot-wearing opponents. We had already seen lots of children kicking soft maize-bag balls with their tough little bare feet. What I could not imagine was no-studs versus studs. Or, as was the case here, the effect of a full-on tackle between three strong players, one of whom is wearing boots, one wearing trainers and one with bare feet. Mr Kwsowa was going to need every last bit of tact and experience to sort this one out.

Ah, we are off again. The problem appears to have been resolved and no one has been sent off, although a yellow card has been held up and there is a good deal of booing. Judging from the frenzied drum dance on the other side of the field, one side are very happy about the decision.

A big difference

This exuberance is what is making the whole day such a totally wonderful experience. We may think we have perfected the art of football support in this country with our anthems and chants and scarves and Mexican waves. Here, on this uneven pitch where the goals have no nets and more than half the players have no boots, they have taken it to another level. Every time there is a shot at goal the hopeful team's support band begins the victory chant, men and women dancing in exuberant chains along and across the touchline. Hanging precariously from trees and perched high on termite hills, the crowds assembled on these natural football terraces join in with singing and whistling and a great deal of standing up and bottom-wiggling.

Adrian is enthralled with the standard of the football.

"They're amazingly good, you know," he whispers. "So fast. And the shooting is very accurate."

"oooooOOOH!"

The drums are going full pelt.

"Well done, Mr Thomas Kasuba, sir. Our Development Manager. Life is for living, is that not true, Mr Kasuba? He has scored a magnificent goal. A goal against AIDS. We will win in the battle against AIDS!"

The whistle has gone for half-time, and suddenly I am aware of one major difference between the match we have been watching and similar events back at home. Besides a few little bags of popcorn, sold for 100 kwacha per bag, there has not been a single item of food in sight. No pies and peas. No burgers squelchy with fried onions. No hot dogs held up to mouths in serviettes with tomato sauce dripping down chins from leaky bread rolls. No fast-food stalls at all. No beer. No cans of Coke. No mess of sweet wrappers. No well-nourished children clamouring for more than they actually need.

The hundreds of people crowding around this field have one thing in common, whichever team they support or are part of. They have probably not eaten since arriving early in the morning, and they will probably not eat until they return home in the evening. I look at the sea of small children. Many of them are, as always, standing yards away, staring fixedly at us now that there is a pause in the football. They have no food that we can see. I look at the teams in their mid-match huddles. They have played with immense energy. What nourishment have they taken into their systems today?

A carnival certainly, but without food. That is a big difference.

Second half

A: So far, my role in the Sports for Life day has been a blessedly passive one. My only formal task has been to lead Fordson and Rodrick as we shook hands an hour ago with every member of the two football teams, Lubuto in the green kit and Kakolo in the yellow, a few minutes before they were due to face each other in the grand final. The idea was for all the players to line up on the pitch in front of the judges' area so that this ritual could take place with due ceremony. I indicated my willingness to fulfil this function when they asked me, being diseased with politeness, but it did feel a little embarrassing. I had never done such a thing before, and who was I to be shaking hands with them, anyway?

I think it went more or less all right. You can role-play almost anything if you have to. I made my way along the row, gripping 22 hands warmly, remembering to use the traditional Zambian handshake, clasping the hand first and then the thumb. I gazed into 44 eyes manfully, and greeted each individual player with the grunt of vague encouragement and exhortation that I have always assumed people in this situation are obliged to produce.

Totally inexplicable to the players, of course.

'Who exactly is this,' I fancied I could hear them asking in their minds as I passed along the line, 'this strange, bearded giant we have never seen before, who seems to have taken it upon himself to fulfil the same role with us as Princess Anne does with the Scottish Rugby Union side?'

Although, when I think about it, I suppose they are unlikely to have heard of Princess Anne, or Rugby Union for that matter. But you know what I mean.

Anyway, as I said, it was not too bad in the end. With characteristic politeness they tolerated the fact that I had briefly delayed the first piercing blast of Mr Kwsowa's whistle, and they were soon sprinting away to take up their positions on the field as I retired to the comfort of my seat beneath the awning.

Now the second half is well under way, and my goodness, these young men can play! Whether with boots, without boots or wearing trainers, they move and turn and run and pass and dribble with all the verve and energy of top-class footballers.

Towards the end of the match, with drums, whistles and voices creating an undulating surge of noise around the pitch, the score has reached two goals to one in favour of the Greens, and time is running out for the tired Yellows. Then, just as the Green supporters are beginning to break into an intensified cacophony of premature celebration – disaster! A Green player deliberately handles the ball in the penalty box. Blatant foul! Uproar!

The referee, his face professionally expressionless, fumbles in his pocket for an instant before withdrawing his hand and thrusting his arm high into the air, the dreaded red card held aloft between finger and thumb. The offender argues feebly for a few moments before giving up and slinking miserably away, head down, arms drooping at his sides. Pocketing the card, Mr Kwsowa turns and points dramatically at the penalty spot.

Penalty! Penalty! Penalty to the Yellows! A chance to equalize. Such excitement!

A very cool young man steps up to take it. The goalkeeper does a few little stretches and practice springs on his goal line, then settles down in a crouch, eyes narrowed and fixed firmly on the penalty-taker. A sudden hush. The Yellow player takes a breath, then trots lightly and with a slightly curving run towards his target. The ball is struck. It is a classic penalty. Easy when you know how. The goalkeeper guesses one way, the striker checks for one infinitesimal moment before directing his shot calmly into the opposite corner. The ball has crossed the goal line.

Goal! Goal! Goal to the Yellows!

Kakolo supporters erupt like a volcano, for now the scores are level. Two goals each, and only minutes left in the game. The Yellow players have shed that weary feeling now. Their heads are up and they are pushing hard towards the Green goal. Supporters of both sides scream and drum and shout.

One last goal! Come on, Yellows! Come on, Greens! One last goal!

Yellows create a good chance to score. A lofted, beautifully accurate pass from the touchline into the penalty area finds the side of a Yellow head and is deflected towards the goal. It is straight. It is too straight. The keeper almost loses his balance, but he manages to stay on his feet and hold on tight to the ball that has thumped directly into his hands. He puffs his cheeks out with relief, and a few seconds later, as the ball once more sails into midfield, the final whistle sounds. The match is over. The teams have drawn, and the result will have to be decided by a penalty shoot-out. Each team will have five shots at goal, and the one that scores the most penalties will win the trophy.

Shoot-out!

Few things are more genuinely, tensely dramatic than a penalty shoot-out, whether it happens in the semi-final of the World Cup in some vast international stadium, or in the least-distinguished amateur tournament held in the tiniest village in the most far-flung corner of the remotest country in the world. The nature of the drama is satisfyingly simple. There is the goal. There is the goalkeeper. There is the ball. There, one by one, are the penalty-takers. Will they score or will they not? Nerves are strained. Teeth are clenched. Palms are sweaty.

Somewhere in the background, children and adults beat out an unremittingly urgent rhythm on their home-made drums as the two teams make their way to the centre line, and the goalkeeper for Kakolo, the Yellow team, marches stiffly toward the netless goalposts at one end of the football field. The ball is placed on its spot by Mr Kwsowa, and the first penalty-taker for the Greens, his manner grave but focused, makes the long walk from the centre of the pitch to the penalty area. The referee raises his whistle to his lips. There is a brief, anticlimactic pause as a very small girl at the edge of the crowd, perhaps puzzled as to why everything seems to have stopped, makes a break for it. Dashing with unself-conscious glee onto the pitch in front of the goal, she jumps over the ball, runs a few wobbling steps, elbows high, forearms beating the air to maintain her balance, then stops and turns delightedly with the obvious intention of repeating the experience. She is thwarted when a big person hurriedly looms, scoops her up and removes her.

The whistle is blown and the first penalty is taken.

Goal! Goal to the Greens! The successful player is so relieved that he can hardly persuade his failing legs to carry him back to where his companions are sprawled on the halfway line.

After two shots each, the teams are still level. No one has yet failed to score. The Greens are equally successful with their third attempt, but disaster strikes for the Yellows when their third penalty-taker sends the ball flying over the bar and into the scrub behind the goal. He buries his face in his hands, distraught beyond words. Dragging his tired body back to the middle, he sinks miserably to the ground. Fellow players pat him on the arms and shoulders. They comfort him and tell him it doesn't matter. But it does matter. It matters to him! Lubuto has taken the lead!

By now the noise is truly deafening. It intensifies when the Greens miss their next shot. Greens are leading by three goals to two, and when the fourth Yellow player fails in his bid to bring the sides level a few minutes later, the score remains unchanged.

Here is drama indeed. If the Greens manage to score with their final attempt, that will be the end of the match. Most of the players on the two teams can hardly bear to watch. They are staring fixedly at the ground or covering their eyes. Once more the referee's whistle manages to pierce through all the competing sounds that are thronging the air. The fifth Green penalty-taker eyes the goal steadily before loping easily towards the ball. He strikes it cleanly with the side of his foot but sends it straight into the arms of the incredulous, immensely relieved goalkeeper.

Despair and jubilation abound. So nearly a victory for the Greens, so close to a defeat for the Yellows. The teams have scored three goals each, and now there has to be an extra shoot-out to determine who has won.

"No one should have to lose ..."

"It's a silly way to decide a match ..."

"Why can't they give the trophy to both teams ..."

They say the same things in Zambia on these occasions as they do anywhere else in the world. And they are right, of course. It is silly.

Mr Kwsowa, however, is not interested in the philosophy of penalty shoot-outs. He has a match to finish. Each team will now have three shots each and, as before, the winner will be awarded the trophy.

There is another short delay as children of various ages, excited by the idea of actually treading the ground on which such an Olympian battle is being fought, run onto the pitch and dance around the penalty area in a fever of excitement. Matters are further complicated by the reappearance of the local drunk, who enters stage right, like some character in one of those very early, rather theatrical Laurel and Hardy films. He is a tall, bonelessly inebriated individual, who, in the tedious manner of drunks the world over, has taken it upon himself to assume stern, tottering responsibility for something that has absolutely nothing to do with him. He tacks unsteadily onto the pitch, listing a little to port, wagging his stick threateningly at empty spaces where scuttling children have just been. They dodge him with ease as they relish the sensation of zipping around the area in front of the goal. It all takes a little while to sort out, but finally, children, drunks and anyone else who shouldn't be there have been tactfully removed, and the final stage of the drama can begin.

I cannot wait to witness the outcome of this titanic struggle. I am on the edge of the crowd, straining to see every detail of the action. Suddenly our friend Charity is at my shoulder, wanting to show me samples of the materials that she and some of the other women produce for sale. Oh, please, not now! They are beautiful, but the second phase of the shoot-out is imminent! I am reminded of my mother-in-law, a lady I miss very much, but who had one fatal flaw. Like Charity, she was quite unable to grasp the fact that you simply cannot interrupt sporting drama for anything less than a life-or-death crisis. My politeness warring with my impatience, I tell Charity that I would love to see and buy some of her work on another day. She nods and smiles and turns away. Something tells me that she will hold me to my promise.

As I turn quickly back towards the pitch Mr Kwsowa blows his whistle to signal the start of the second shoot-out, and the first penalty-taker begins his run. It is an accurate shot. Greens have scored with their first attempt. Yellows fail with theirs. Greens are successful with their second shot at goal, and so are Yellows. If Greens score with their third attempt the match is over. Over on the centre line, all of the Green players are on their feet now. Holding hands, swinging their arms rhythmically backwards and forwards, they lean almost imperceptibly towards the goal, seeking to express and transmit solidarity with their chosen representative as he trudges like a sacrificial lamb to the place of sudden glory or prolonged agony. Now he is preparing to take his shot. Now he is running towards the ball. Now he strikes it firmly, low and to the right. The goalkeeper has guessed rightly this time, throwing himself to his left, but he is out of luck. It is a matter of inches. The ball passes under his outstretched left arm. The blast of the whistle sounds for the last time. Greens have scored! Lubuto have won the match by three goals to one in the second penalty shoot-out, and the trophy will be theirs.

Sad Yellows. Radiant Greens race down the pitch to embrace their hero of the moment, each other and anyone else who happens to be standing nearby. An outstanding football match with a tense, enthralling finish, and a fitting end to this wonderful day.

Prizes

But Sports for Life day is not quite over yet. One more vitally important thing has to happen before we all go home, and that is the distribution of prizes and trophies. No one wants to miss this sizzlingly joyful item on the agenda. Within minutes the entire crowd has thronged to the side of the football pitch in front of the judges' awning, jostling, pushing and shoving to get as close to the heart of the action as they can. A small semicircular area is left clear for the winning teams to use when they approach the presentation table.

It is not large enough, someone in authority protests loudly, the crowd is just going to have to draw back and create more space. The crowd, conforming to the behaviour of all crowds since the earliest recorded history of crowds, shows scant interest in co-operating with this request, but they have reckoned without one crucial factor. They have reckoned without the Scouts.

Now is the time for this well-drilled body of youngsters to come into their own. Following a succession of briskly barked orders from their red-gloved leader, they duck and burrow their way through the masses, emerging eventually to form a human chain around the space in front of the presentation table. They hold their white sticks horizontally, using them like portable railings to press back the crowd until it grudgingly gives up a metre or two of ground. It is an impressively conducted campaign. Some of these lads really are only pint-sized, but they are resolutely confident. Orders are orders, and right is on their side. They may do their duty with an air of military rectitude, but I suspect that this is just their official mien. Their eyes are shining now that they are involved in an important job that really does need to be done. They are having a great time.

Unexpectedly I am once more pressed into duty, and so is Bridget. I am to present the prizes and trophies, and Bridget is to do lots of beaming, handshaking and congratulating. I feel much happier about it this time. There is an all-inclusive atmosphere of celebration and excitement around the presentation table. I hardly think the winners are going to be very bothered about who gives them their awards, just so long as they get them.

There are four or five of us stationed behind the table, including Rodrick and Fordson. They will hand me the prizes as the teams come up, prizes that range from 275,000 kwacha for the winners of the football, down to 50,000 kwacha for the fifth-placed teams. In addition to the trophy for the winning netball and football sides, each player will also receive a small plaque to commemorate his or her participation in the tournament.

The crowds have been compressed into a solid mass by the Scouts at the front, and by the people who stubbornly refuse to be pushed any further away from the action at the back. The effect is of one giant block of dark wood carved into hundreds of head and face shapes at its top end.

A hush falls as the formal proceedings begin. Each separate presentation follows the same pattern. There is a serious silence and stillness as individual results are announced, followed by a disintegration of the solid block into waving, dancing component parts, and a wild eruption of applause and celebration as the competitors approach the table. The giant jigsaw then reassembles itself in preparation for the next award.

The girls from the netball teams, beginning with the various runners-up and followed by the tournament winners, are the first to receive their cash and their trophies. Members of the victorious team approach the table in a sort of conga, their blue, white and orange shirts swinging on their hips as they chassé joyfully towards the presentation party to receive congratulations and awards. As Rose Keleto, captain of the winning team, leaves the table she thrusts her arms into the air in uncomplicated elation, trophy in one hand, green envelope containing prize money of 250,000 kwacha (about £30) in the other, twin symbols of victory in a land where success is rare and deserves to be celebrated. And celebrate it they will. At some point in the very near future the netball team will use this prize money to throw a party, and what a party that is likely to be. You will find no girls standing miserably around waiting to dance in this part of the world.

The dignified Mr Kwsowa receives an award in recognition of his sterling work as referee, and then the football teams receive theirs. The boys are less openly exuberant than the girls perhaps, but they convey through their expressions and body language that participation and success in this event mean a very great deal.

Finally, the ceremony ends and the crowd begins to disperse. After a few minutes there is only dust where all those people were standing just a short time ago. This dust is everywhere here. In fact, it seems to us that it is only possible to view the world of Zamtan through a thin cloud of dust. When the dust of this day has settled as much as it ever will, I suspect that Rodrick and the other members of the committee will feel that it has been a good time for the community. People of all ages have come together. They have laughed and cheered and gossiped and hopefully received a little boost to their belief that they really do belong to one another. Just as importantly, through posters, discussions and Rodrick's extraordinary sports commentary, the message of caution and warning about HIV/AIDS has been communicated and reinforced. It is only one more small step in the dance of life, but most of us are only able to learn small steps, one at a time.

As we close our notebooks and prepare to leave, the bit at the end of the twenty-fifth chapter of Matthew's Gospel pops into my mind, and it occurs to me that there will be another award ceremony one day, in a quite different setting, where there is no dust and no food shortage and not even a trace of the deadly virus. Those who have worked and fought and helped and con-tributed towards the battle against disease and poverty will be called up, much to their own surprise, to receive congratulations and thanks for the effort they have made. Don't ask me who those people will be. I can guess at a few of them, but I hope the list will get longer and longer in the years to come. I don't even know if those who perform this final celebratory conga will be expected to use the African or the English handshake. All I can say for certain sure, is that it will not be me giving out the prizes.

An alien in Kitwe

A: It is the little things that tend to take you aback. For instance, Bridget and I were free the afternoon after the Sports for Life finals, and we decided to explore Kitwe, the city where our guest house was located. Kitwe (pronounced 'kit-way'), the second largest city in Zambia and once the heart of the copper-mining industry, is not large by British standards, but it was relaxing to take an hour or two out from our planned schedule to stroll the half-mile or so of wide, dusty road that eventually took us into the centre of town. The only real shop in Zamtan is Rodrick's small establishment, its stock limited in variety and quantity because of financial restraints. Here in the middle of the city a selection of shops, including one extremely well-stocked supermarket, offered customers just about anything they might want or think they needed – assuming, of course, that they had the money to pay for it.

In one of the side streets we happened upon a second-hand bookshop. I am not quite sure why this should have surprised me so much. I think it was something to do with the fact that, up to now, we had been focusing so intensely on a situation where there was never a surplus amount of anything, money or food. Parting with actual cash in exchange for a second-hand book seemed, just for a moment, too silly for words. Ridiculous, of course. Why shouldn't people have access to cheap books? A very economical form of entertainment, apart from anything else. One of my favourite activities is rooting through the dark caverns and canyons of those shops where you get the distinct feeling that the ceiling would fall in if you interfered with the wrong column of redundant encyclo-paedias.

As it turned out, there wasn't a great deal that was of interest in this particular shop. Most of the books were laid out in rows on long shelves so that their front covers were visible to customers. It didn't take long to establish that there was nothing we really wanted. Then, just when we had almost completed our circuit of the long, rectangular shop space, Bridget raised her hand and pointed to a splash of crimson on one of the shelves.

"Look, Adrian," she said, her voice high with surprise, "there's your book! What's it doing in Kitwe?"

There indeed was my book, or one of my books. *An Alien at St Wilfred's*, which I wrote some years ago, is a work of fiction describing the visit of a small, angel-like figure to an ordinary high street church, and the effect of his presence on four key figures, including the vicar.

Many of my books have been translated into other languages, and they certainly travel into distant parts of the English-speaking world, but for some reason the sight of that red cover on a shelf in a shop in Kitwe was a real shock. It was just there. My book. Far from home. Looking wistfully at me from the shelf like a child who has been lost and wants to be taken home.

"Look," I said to the lady behind the counter, "that's my book!"

"No it is not," she replied, "it is mine."

Nonplussed for a moment, I recovered sufficiently to explain that what I meant was that I was the author of the volume, and I added that I would like to buy it. She nodded dispassionately, patently unimpressed, as she took my money and placed the book in a brown paper bag. Real writers wouldn't be going around shops buying their own books, would they? Not successful ones, anyway.

I bought it. I bought my own book. Why did I buy my own book? I told myself that it was because I knew I didn't have a copy of that particular edition, the one with the red cover. And that is factually true. The real reason, though, loony as it might seem, was this. The sight of my little book reminded me that I really do exist, even in Zambia. I wanted to take that reminder with me. There you are. Make of it what you will. Each of us is poor in our own way.

7. Sunday Best

A: "Oh, Father, you love your people. It is a lov-er-ly day because you love us!"

Mwalusi Silumba's deep, passionate voice rolls across the heads of his attentive congregation, up to heaven, and out into the fresh, sparkling African morning. In addition to Peter, Fordson, Thom, Jim, Bridget and myself, we have counted 30 women, 26 men and over 40 children crowded into his church this morning. Most are seated on wooden benches. We, the outsiders, guests of honour yet again, have been placed on white plastic chairs, arranged in a row against the side wall near the table that serves as an altar. This table is covered with a cloth that may be of dubious quality, but which is somehow so brilliantly pure and white in intention that it shimmers like silver in the half-light.

The building we are occupying is what people in England would probably describe as a barn-like structure, mostly built of stone but with a boarded, heavily patched roof, supported by rough wooden struts. Inside it is dark but dappled, the bright, dust-bearing winter sunshine pouring through small triangular holes cut into the walls at regular intervals, as well as through two doors, one at each end of the building.

For today's service Mwalusi Silumba, pastor to the Zamtan Methodist congregation, is wearing a white shirt, light blue tie, a rust-coloured jacket and light grey trousers. It is hard to estimate his age, but after a brief, whispered discussion we guess that he might be in his early sixties. Dignified, tall and slim to the point of emaciation, with wide eyes and handsome, sculpted features, he conveys that sense, peculiar to those who habitually draw close to God, of seeming to have spotted something important in the far distance that is invisible to the rest of us. Pastor Silumba appears very steady within himself, and rather serious in demeanour until, when some of the children turn and look to him for approval after finishing one of their songs, a ready smile of appreciation lights up his face. Early in the service he publicly introduces his much younger, very cheerfully disposed wife to the congregation. It is only a moment, and few words are said, but we can see that these two people are immensely proud of each other.

So far this Sunday has been a good experience for us. Visitors are usually met with a shake of the hand and lots of warmth at the door of our church in Hailsham, but never as we were greeted this morning. As we drove off the main Kitwe road and parked in front of the church building we were able to see the entire congregation lined up in the clear space outside the church, singing, dancing and clapping their hands as they waited to welcome us to their service. Nothing sombre about this crowd. Most people were wearing their Sunday best, that was obvious, but it was a long way removed from the tediously dull 'best' that still characterizes some of the church gatherings in our own country. Many of the women were brightly arrayed, a good number of them wearing circular, wide-rimmed straw boaters with coloured ribbons around the crowns. A recent G.I.K. delivery, perhaps?

That sense of being involved in a television 'soap' was even more pronounced on this occasion. There, as we began our procession along the line of smiling men and women, was Rose, captain of the victorious netball team, a strikingly attractive woman, vividly dressed in yellow and blue, her face alight with the joy of Sunday morning. There also was our friend David, committee member and husband to Elizabeth, the lady in charge of the pigs, and adoptive father of Penelope, my little friend with the huge smile. There were others we recognized, and they all greeted us with genuine enthusiasm, but the most openly demonstrative of all was Femmy, substitute mother to so many suffering souls in her role as a caregiver. Femmy was not content with a simple hand-shake and a smile when we reached her place in the line. She threw her arms first around Bridget and then around me, whirling us round in a little dance of celebration.

A few minutes later, comparing notes after entering the church, Bridget and I agreed that the spontaneity and generous warmth of this welcome from the family of God had meant a great deal to us. And I know why this was. It was because we had been allowed to experience for the first time a sense of genuinely belonging, albeit in a very small way, to people from the community in which we had spent such a comparatively short time. Being known. Being recognized. That is what made it so special.

Impressions of the service. So many, striking us like the shafts of sunshine that continually strike hair, hands, hats, seats and patches on the wall, creating startling little pools of light in the midst of darkness and randomly illuminating the still, entranced faces of children.

Those children. Their special time for singing and dancing is near the beginning of the service. They put every last ounce of energy into it, gleefully employing arms and legs and heads and shoulders with an instinctive, unconscious professionalism that simply engages with the rhythm of rightness. Bouncing and rocking and throwing their weight from one side to the other, they spare nothing of their bodies or their voices as a lady of the church leads them in simple songs and chants of worship and praise, the most exuberant being: "When the Son of God is dancing, the devil can't come near ..."

Bridget and I watch and learn. That is what we have always done with children. Except you become like one of these, Jesus said, you cannot enter the kingdom of heaven. It is neither a fruitless nor an irksome study.

Greetings and introductions. All of us visitors stand to speak a few words, Peter catching his head on one of the low beams as he makes his way from the back of the church where he has been operating his video camera. Our own churches will be assembling at this very moment, we tell the congregation, distant brothers and sisters who are all members of the same body that is gathered here this morning, the body of Christ. It is a privilege to be here, and we greet them on behalf of the churches in England, and in America, where Jim, our photographer, is now living with his family.

Reciprocal greetings from the pastor.

"These visitors from far places," he says, "have come as a reminder that God loves us. They have come," he adds, with a smile in Peter's direction and a sudden flash of humour, "even though it means they bang their heads to get here."

I ask myself if it can really be true that we are reminders of God's love to these people. A wonderful thought. And too warming to dismiss. Oh, all right then, we are.

Songs from congregation and choir. As men, women and children raise their voices to God I collect bits and pieces of translation from Fordson, who is sitting on my right. I am sure he would much rather be joining in wholeheartedly with the singing than whispering meanings of songs to me, but he is as willing as ever. I jot the fragments down.

"Instead of sinning, come to God. Life is borrowed from God, so be careful with it."

"God, you are good! You are so good that I have to say thank you."

"When he comes there will be dancing, the angels will dance with us."

"I pray every day to Father and Son, and I know one day they will answer."

"I'm singing for the Lord, who is alive!"

"Lay your burden down on the cross of Christ," sings the choir, "lay it down, lay it down." The simple, beautifully sung chorus is repeated again and again, as the singers place their Bibles on their heads and then smilingly sweep them away to symbolize the removal of burdens. One of the ladies in the choir has a sleeping baby on her back. The child's head bobs and sways in time to the music as his mother dances and sings. "Lay it down, lay it down. Lay it down, lay it down. Lay your burden down on the cross of Christ."

The still centre

Collection

There is a significant tradition in Christian poetry and philosophy of discovering a still place at the centre of existence. Deep in the very heart of faith, or life, or our experience of God, there is a point that does not turn while all other things turn. It is relaxation within restlessness, it is resolution and calm at the hub of ever-circling questions and concerns. It is something to do with the promise of peace. For me, quite unexpectedly, the still point of this service is the collection, or, more accurately, the person who has been entrusted with receiving offerings from the congregation. This is, inevitably I suppose, a child. A boy of eight or nine years has been handed the silver-painted, woven bowl into which the money will be placed. From the moment when this receptacle is placed into his hands, the child becomes a living statue. He wears the mantle of his responsibility with the grave concentration of one who has been entrusted with a task that might affect the future of the world. Four-square and steady he stands, as vulnerable and as powerful as Jesus, who neither demands nor grasps anything that is possessed by men and women but simply waits quietly for them to voluntarily bring their gifts to him.

The pastor approaches first, dropping his offering into the bowl as the choir begins to sing. A lady follows him. She is holding a very small child. She closes her baby's fist around the few crumpled currency notes that she has brought, and then prises it open so that the money falls into the silver bowl. It is a shared offering. God will understand. One by one the members of the congregation bring their financial loaves and fishes to the front. Quite a few 'mites' here, and not just from widows.

All have given now. Surrendering his bowl and his responsibility, the child slips quietly away to take his seat in the half-light. The pastor prays over the money, and the collection is completed.

Love is foremost

The reading. A passage from the fourth chapter of Peter's first epistle.

The end of all things is near. Therefore be clear minded and self-controlled so that you can pray. Above all, love each other deeply, because love covers over a multitude of sins. Offer hospitality to one another without grumbling. Each one should use whatever gift he has received to serve others, faithfully administering God's grace in its various forms. If anyone speaks, he should do it as one speaking the very words of God. If anyone serves, he should do it with the strength God provides, so that in all things God may be praised through Jesus Christ. To him be the glory and the power for ever and ever. (NIV)

A song before the sermon.

"I'll never forget the message of the Lord ..."

The sermon.

It begins with a story set in the bush, and it features animals as characters. The snake is the devil. Jesus, rather surprisingly, is a rat, but, of course, a good and loving rat. The message of the story and the sermon is love for one another. God did not abandon man when he first sinned because he had mercy and love. Without that love and mercy we die. We need love. We must be hospitable without grumbling. We need to preach and serve and love one another. We have God's love, so what can stop us? We will see Jesus in our midst. All good things come from God. The love of God must be fulfilled in us. We will love and help each other. We will provide for each other, for all those who hunger and thirst. Faith, hope and love are listed by Paul in Corinthians, but love is the most important – love is foremost. Amen.

The final prayer is delivered by Fordson in passionate pentecostal style. He stands to face the congregation, his arms rising and circling and falling as he unconsciously mimes the whole needy world being enclosed in the embrace of God.

"Help your people to know that which you want them to do. Father, if you are for us, no one should be against us. Father, I want to speak against every power of the enemy that would be fashioned against this church. In Jesus' mighty name, Father, that they will be under the feet of the mighty Lord Jesus Christ. We sprinkle the blood of Christ on every member of this church. I pray that, God, you alone will help them. You alone shall encourage them. You alone shall give them this fresh love.

"Father, I want to pray for the members of the families represented here, that you alone, oh God, should be with them. Cause them to love you, oh God, to be a shining example of God in their lives, in Jesus' mighty name. Father God, as we are going to leave, one from another, I pray that you alone should be ahead of us and before us. We know that the devil is like a roaring lion, but, Father, we know that we are more than conquerors in your name. Receive the praise and glory, Father. We pray you, Lord, into the rest of the day, so that you alone are in our lives. Amen!"

Fordson's rousing prayer culminates in a round of applause from the congregation, and the service is over. A song of farewell is sung as we file out into the sunshine. We discover that this church has its own special way of saying goodbye. The first person to exit greets the second person, who then lines up ready to greet the third person, who, in his or her turn, joins the line ready to salute the fourth person, and so on. By this means every member of the congregation shakes hands with every other person who has been present during the morning. It's a wonderful idea, and one that we feel might be well worth introducing to churches in the United Kingdom – weather and willingness to change permitting, that is. It occurs to us that, of those two obstacles, the weather will probably prove less of a problem.

As we climb into the World Vision vehicle for our drive back into Kitwe, the words of that one children's song in particular are going round and round in our heads.

"When the Son of God is dancing, the devil can't come near ..."

Bridget and I so want to be part of making it possible for the Son of God to dance here in Zambia. You can help. We can all help. We want him to dance as exuberantly as those children did just now. We want him to dance with the ineffable joy that springs from a knowledge that Christian people are genuinely willing to be his hands and feet and voice in a country, and among a people, where the devil has been far too near for far too long.

My most embarrassing moment

B: With a sense of joy at being alive and part of God's wider family, I greeted the pastor after the service. It was indeed turning out to be a lov-er-ly day. Rarely had I sensed the Spirit of God moving as I had in this little church. Never had I been part of such committed and energetic worship. So I was surprised to see him looking a little sad.

"I wish to apologize for the many of our congregation who arrived at the service rather late."

"Oh, please, please don't worry," I replied, with what I hoped was an affirming smile, "loads of us turn up late for church in England every Sunday."

He looked genuinely puzzled.

"But I had understood," he responded gravely, "that all people in your country had clocks in their homes."

8. Facing the Future

B: The guest house where we stayed in Kitwe was comfortably informal and a nice place to wind down when the evening came. It was there, over a drink, that we were at last able to talk further with Fordson Kafwetu about his involvement here.

"The thing is, Fordson," said Adrian, "I happen to know that you have an engineering degree. How on earth did you come to be running Zamtan ADP?"

"Well, Adrian, I want to begin by mentioning to you something that happened to me a few years ago now. It is true that I have an engineering degree, but I had been feeling restless in the work I was doing. So one day I said a prayer to God. I said, 'Lord, use me as a channel for your Spirit.' Nothing happened immediately, but I was not really surprised as I didn't know what I was asking God for. Then I found that everyone I came into contact with began to contribute something to my thinking, and God began to open doors in my life. Somehow I moved into community care. Do you wish me to continue?"

Of course we did. We settled down to hear more of what made this intriguing man tick.

"I was very excited to be working at last in the lives of human beings. To see change, to actually see people move from one level to another is what now motivates me. As World Vision workers we meet people who are feeling hopeless in their lives because they have discovered that they have HIV/AIDS. Now, when we can become involved we are able to say, 'This is not the end of the world. We can work together and help you to gather your life and be able to forge ahead.'

"This inspires me and I thank God every day that I made this decision.

"But, you know, I learnt much of what I know from one woman. I was waiting to take part in a radio programme in Kitwe, and she too was waiting. I think it was to speak on another programme. Anyway, I noticed that she was wearing the red ribbon, and I asked her what was her understanding of this ribbon. We only had a short while to talk, but from my first meeting I knew she was a very special person. So I arranged to speak with her again and this time we had two hours. I learnt of her story."

Princess of hope

"Princess (you understand that is simply her given name) Kasune Zulu had lost her baby sister and both her parents to HIV/AIDS by the time she was only fourteen years old. With two younger brothers to look after,

Princess married an older man with a steady income only to find, at the age of twenty-one, that she too had the virus. Instead of feeling despairing, Princess felt that God was calling her to go out and educate others. She even hitch-hiked with truckers in order to tell them how to prevent the spread of AIDS and hosted a radio show called 'Living Positively'. What I immediately saw in her was hope, and I thought if we could only tap into this hope we could give so much to our people who are sick with HIV/AIDS. So I asked her to come and work with us in Zamtan. Her time as our assistant development facilitator was wonderful for us. She inspired many, many people. She says to the sick, 'You don't want to die before you are dead.' She is, you know, a big personality. Very strong. Very colourful. Very passionate. With a big smile and a big laugh. Then one day I felt God was telling me to introduce her to the national office so she could be an inspiration to many programmes in Zambia. Now she is an advocate for us all over the world and, do you know, the president of the United States once sent a message to say he 'needed' to see her. When he met her he gave her a kiss and she cried and told him that the tears were 'the tears of millions of children around the world'. Apparently she didn't want to wash her face for a week! We have a picture of that kiss in our office. It makes us smile. She has visited England and spoken to many assemblies there, and I believe there were even articles about her published in your newspapers. I think you met her, Adrian, while she was in London. You will agree that Princess always tells things as they are and her Christianity is very practical, very robust. She will say, 'A man is infected by HIV and his wife is not. Should he sleep with her unprotected, so she becomes infected? Now what sort of God would make people do a silly thing like that?' She makes people laugh, but she also makes them think. Recently she was part of a gathering of world leaders in Bangkok. So now she is a very important person, but what most impressed me then and now is her ability to empower people with hope."

The importance of empowerment

"Empowerment of all sorts is, we believe at World Vision, very, very important. In fact, I see the most important aspect of my job as helping these local guys learn about leadership and management. And supporting them psychologically. You see, we can organize many things to help a community, but if the local people are not empowered then when the time comes for us to leave, after maybe 15 years, the initiatives will not continue. But when the local community is involved with the decision making and the management of programmes, then they will continue after we go.

"Take the leaders in the churches. You saw this morning how loving the message was that Pastor Silumba delivered. How he told us that God did not abandon us when we sinned. How we must serve and care for each other. A few years ago that would not have necessarily been the message. Church members were frightened to tell their leaders that they had HIV/AIDS because they knew they would be judged as sinners and excluded from their church. Well, we at World Vision knew that in Zambia the church has a huge influence over how people think and act, so we encouraged an interdenominational committee to be established with the aim of finding a common strategy to prevent the spread of HIV/AIDS. Each church in the area, whatever the denomination, was asked to supply six members for that committee. Then we arranged for these people to go for training to learn how important it is to lift the old taboos about speaking about sex, and how, because of their influential role in people's lives, Christians need to be in the forefront of the fight against the spread of the disease. As soon as they understood, they accepted that their message needed to change. They still preach salvation through faith, tell people about Jesus Christ and advocate abstinence. But they also make it clear that there is no stigma attached to contracting the virus. Instructions in the book of James about caring for widows and orphans are central to their preaching. It is very exciting to see how successful the churches have been in turning the tide against discrimination and towards love and acceptance."

Adrian leans forward. I know exactly what he is going to ask.

"Fordson, we heard a song written by the headmistress at the school we visited that worried us a bit."

Adrian thumbs through his tattered notebook until he finds the relevant page. "Ah yes, here it is:

World Vision care for us

Look at us as your children

Look at us orphans

World Vision who is our father

Please help us.

"What we wanted to ask you is whether this is how you want the community to see you – as someone they can depend on? A paternal providing figure in their lives? I would have thought that ..."

Fordson interrupts him gently, unfazed by the question.

"Adrian, this is how I see it. When a child is young he depends on his father to carry him. When he can walk on his own he will need less help, and when he is older he will take charge of his life. At the moment the people of

Zamtan are very dependent on us, but increasingly they are stepping out on their own.

"Taking over responsibility like this means that orphans and vulnerable children will continue to be supported after World Vision leaves the area to help another group of villages elsewhere. We can be confident that houses will continue to be built. Grandparents who have to take an extra burden in their old age will be supported. Young people will be educated. The sick will be cared for. All this will be done by members of the community themselves. And we hope that, by the time we leave Zamtan, they will have the infrastructure to make these things possible. We have already built a health clinic and housing for the nurses. Also a school and teachers' housing. We are at present managing the building of a new community centre.

"You know, this disease, HIV/AIDS, has the potential for wiping us out. It has caused us all great pressure. I myself have my wife's sister and children living with us. It is not easy for any of us. We have seen the worst poverty we have ever experienced because of the disease. We see many children suffering very much. Sometimes they are looking after sick parents and they feel they cannot bear it any longer. We are there to help them carry their burden. But we can do very little if we are not supported with money. You in the developed countries are helping us to change their lives. You are giving them hope. On their behalf I thank you for that."

Birdseed

A: It was good to sit and listen to Fordson. One of the things that we greatly appreciated about this man was his spontaneous response to the areas of need that we saw in his company. A lesser man might have tried to give the impression of being casually aware of every shade and aspect of things going on in the areas where members of his team were working. Not so Fordson, in whom energetic curiosity and practical compassion were present in equal measure. This was the case, for instance, with his reaction to the answer that we continually heard when we asked what the greatest problem of all was for the people of Zamtan.

Food. It was always about lack of food. The hunger that will not allow you to focus on anything else until your stomach is able to send a message to your brain to say that the situation has improved and other things can be considered.

The World Vision team and the Zamtan committee are, quite rightly, putting their best efforts into establishing projects and initiatives that will be self-sustaining in the long run. This is the most constructive way in which to truly assist a community. In the meantime, people are very hungry. At one point in our journey around the community Fordson, having heard this reply on so many occasions, nodded seriously and spoke of how it is easy to lose sight of immediate need when your attention and planning are so firmly fixed on the future.

The issue of long-term versus immediate need reminds me of an ancient joke that you may have heard before. I repeat it here for obvious reasons.

This story concerns a man who bought a budgerigar in a cage from a pet shop. The man who sold it to him was confident in asserting that the budgie was already learning to speak and would very quickly add more and more words to his vocabulary. The customer returned home happily with his purchase.

Two days later he was back, complaining that the bird had said not a single word since leaving the shop.

The pet shop owner stroked his chin thoughtfully. "Hmm, I tell you what," he said, "he probably needs a little exercise. Why don't you buy one of these little ladders that we sell. Hang it in his cage so he can run up and down when he wants to. That ought to do the trick."

"Okay, I'll try it," said the customer, "wrap it up."

And away he went.

Two days later he was back.

"That budgie you sold me – "

"Oh, yes, the speaking one."

"Well, that's the problem – it's not."

"Not what?"

"It's not a speaking one."

"Still not a word?"

"Nothing."

"Despite the ladder?"

"Well, he certainly did run up and down the ladder. Seemed to enjoy it, but he didn't speak."

The pet shop owner considered for a few moments.

"I'd say he's bored because there's not enough stimulation in his cage," he announced at last. "I've got some little mirrors here that'll probably sort him out. Take one of these. Put it at the bottom of the ladder. He'll be able to look at himself in his mirror then run up and down the ladder a few times, and after that I'm pretty sure he'll start to talk."

The customer paid for the mirror and took it home with him, but two days later he was back in the shop.

"Right," he said, "I put that mirror at the bottom of the ladder like you told me to, and the budgie looked at himself in the mirror and ran up and down the ladder a few times, but he still didn't talk."

"Nothing?"

"Not a word."

"Not even one?"

"Not a peep."

"Okay," said the pet shop owner after a few moments of head scratching. "I'm pretty sure I know the answer. What this budgie of yours needs is to hear some really nice sounds in his cage. Why don't you take one of these little silver bells that we sell here and hang it from the roof of his cage next to the top of the ladder, okay?"

"You think that'll work?"

"Well, he'll look at himself in the mirror, run up and down the ladder and then ring the bell. After that he'll feel so well exercised, and so stimulated, and so entertained by the sound of the bell, that he's bound to start talking."

"I'll try it," said the customer, "wrap it up."

Two days passed.

On the third day the customer returned to the shop yet again. In his hand he was carrying the cage he had bought, still containing the ladder, the mirror and the bell. On the floor of the cage lay the budgie, his eyes closed, his little feet in the air.

There was a short silence as the pet shop owner stared at this tragic sight.

"What happened?" he asked at last.

"Well," said the customer, "I took the bell home with me and I hung it from the roof of the cage next to the top of his ladder, just like you said."

"And?"

"He ran up and down the ladder, he looked at himself in the mirror and he rang his bell. Exactly like you said. Then, when I came downstairs this morning, I found him lying on the bottom of the cage, on the point of death."

"I see. Oh dear. And did he say anything before he died?"

"Yes, he did. In a little gasping voice he said, 'Tell your friend at the pet shop I'd appreciate it if he'd sell you some birdseed...'"

Sir Bob Geldof recently commented that more people in Africa are dying from hunger than from AIDS. It is a timely reminder. Governments like ours are at last looking at ways of tackling the problem of debt, but it seems to be taking a very long time.

Why doesn't the government do more?

B: I have always hated bullies. People who bring misery into the lives of those smaller and more defenceless than themselves. People so thick-skinned that they simply don't care about the suffering they are inflicting. People who have much, taking from people who have next to nothing. Which is why I am so discomfited by everything I have learned about the way Western leaders have dealt with international debt. The defence for my inertia has always been ignorance, so, if you have taken up the same stance, the facts that I discovered when I finally bothered to delve under the surface will probably shock you as much as they did me.

In 1990, Zambia was ranked as one of the most developed countries in sub-Saharan Africa. Now it is one of the poorest. So what happened?

The oil crisis in the early 1970s meant that imports became more expensive. At the same time, the relative collapse of commodity prices meant that revenue from exports was reduced. But there was help at hand – fairy godmothers who could at one wave of their wands dramatically change the fortunes of a country in crisis like Zambia – the World Bank and the International Monetary Fund (IMF). Zambia could borrow US$814 million.

Surely such a generous injection of cash would bring an end to their problems. They could stabilize their economy and, when they were again strong and self-sufficient, they could repay their debt. And all they had to do in return for this generosity was to commit themselves to implementing World Bank- and IMF-endorsed economic policies. Little did they know.

By the end of the 1970s their debt had risen to US$3,244 million, and by 1990 they owed no less than US$6,916 million.

US$814 million to US$6,916 million in twenty years.

More than nine times the amount they had originally borrowed.

Zambia was, of course, not the only poverty-stricken country to find itself in this disastrous situation, and eventually an initiative calling itself Heavily Indebted Poor Countries (HIPC) was created. At last it looked as though they could crawl out of the ditch, wipe themselves down and start again. Not so.

As of 2003, Zambia had received only five per cent of the debt service reduction they had been promised. So serious is the crisis that the Zambian Finance Minister, Peter Magande, fears that even if they receive the full quota of debt relief they will not be able to sustain their debt repayments. To make matters even worse it appears that in return for debt relief, such as it is, Zambia must implement economic policies such as privatization and cuts in public spending that meet with World Bank and IMF approval. Most of these have proved to be dismal failures.

Take, for example, trade liberalization. Lowering tariffs on textile products and removing all tariffs on used clothes have encouraged the import of cheap second-hand clothing from industrialized countries. What can be wrong with that? Surely if Zambians can now buy cheap second-hand clothing that must be a good thing. Well, actually, no. In 1991 there were 140 textile manufacturing firms in Zambia. Now there are eight. A thriving factory in Ndola, for instance, used to employ 250 people. Now it employs 25. Utter disaster.

Then there is the IMF policy for agricultural liberalization, which among other things insisted that government intervention in the agricultural sector be reduced. Well, in 2000 even the World Bank itself admitted that the removal of subsidies on maize and fertilizer had led to 'stagnation and regression', instead of helping Zambia's agricultural sector, and admitted that farmers were left worse off.

But what about privatization? Surely this must have helped to encourage enterprise? Well, if there had not been a one-size-fits-all pattern to the IMF and World Bank programme it may have succeeded, and it is true that the transference of some state-run enterprises into private hands has meant that they are now operating more effectively, but many companies have collapsed, jobs have been lost and welfare programmes discontinued. So fed up have the citizens of Lusaka become that when the government proposed privatizing Zambia's state electricity company (ZESCO) and state bank (ZNCB), they organized a major protest march. The response to this display of public resistance reveals some very troubling facts. The government was swayed into reversing its commitment to selling off these companies. The IMF responded immediately by announcing that Zambia risked forfeiting US$1 billion in debt relief if it did not go ahead with privatization. An IMF representative stated that if they did not sell, they would not get the money.

From my inexpert perspective, the whole thing appears to be a mess. In addition, the IMF seems to have failed in its main aim, which was to stem temporary balance of payment problems. In fact, unbelievably,

Zambia's trade deficit has actually increased. In 1990 the difference between imports and exports was –5 per cent of gross domestic product (GDP), that is the total market value of all final goods and services produced in a given year, equal to total consumer, investment and government spending plus the value of exports, minus the value of imports. What we are looking for, apparently, is growth in GDP. Since 1994, Zambia's GDP has been between –9 per cent and –15 per cent. Even I can see that those statistics mean bad news!

Then there is employment. The list makes depressing reading:

Formal manufacturing employment in 1991 was 75,400. By 1998 it had sunk to 43,320.

Paid employment in manufacturing and mining in 1991 stood at 140,000. In 1998 the number was down to 83,000.

Paid employment in agriculture in 1990 amounted to 78,000. In the year 2000 it was 50,000, reflecting the same downward trend.

Perhaps the most shocking statistic of all is that textile manufacturing employed 34,000 in 1990 but was down to 4,000 by the year 2000.

A total loss of nearly 150,000 jobs in ten years.

And what does this mean in real terms for the people of Zambia? It means there are more very, very hungry folk. It also means there is less likelihood of achieving the Millennium Development Goals (MDGs) by the globally agreed date of 2015 for eradicating hunger, providing primary education for all and reducing child mortality. In other words, it means that Zambia's level of human development is in free fall.

Just as a matter of interest, Zambia's projected budget deficit is less than that of either the US or the UK. The difference is a matter of strength. A UK treasury spokesman said recently that they would not accept a stability pact from the IMF, the European Commission or anyone else. Sadly, poor little Zambia does not have the same luxury of being able to tell the IMF to sling its hook!

It is true that the IMF and the World Bank could argue that the Zambian people chose these policies through their 'participatory' Poverty Reduction Strategy Papers (PRSP) process. On paper that might appear to be so, but in fact the IMF and the World Bank have been unwilling to renegotiate any of their major policies. The undemocratic imposition of policies on Zambia (especially in the area of reduced tariffs on imports) has also undermined Zambia's ability to engage effectively in initiatives such as the World Trade Organization, which was created in 1994. Zambia's bargaining chips have effectively been taken away.

As I said, I hate bullies. I hate big kids taking property from little kids in the playground. The only way to deal with them is to tell the grown-ups and let them exert appropriate discipline. This usually involves giving back whatever has been taken under protest. It will mean fair play.

It is surely time to cancel Zambia's debt and that of all other countries like Zambia. The UK Development Secretary sits on the board of the World Bank. The UK Chancellor of the Exchequer sits on the board of the IMF.

We know about the promises. Hopefully by the time you read this something positive will have taken place, enabling governments of countries like Zambia to be in a position where they can fund initiatives in health and education and social care.

9. Chililabombwe

A: Before this chapter of the book gets going, it might be worth just taking a moment to practise saying the word 'Chililabombwe'. There are two reasons for this. The not-so-good one is that every time the word appears your eye, and therefore your attention, will stumble over it, and that is not a good thing. The other, much better reason for learning how to pronounce the word, is that, properly said, it rolls around your mouth and your mind in a truly satisfying way. A little piece of Africana that you can play with whenever you want, a verbal toy.

So! Chililabombwe. Here is how it breaks down. Just read the following as it appears:

CHILL ILL ER BOM BWAY

A couple of practices and you'll have it off pat. Done it? Good, well done. Enjoy it when you have nothing better to do. Now we can set off.

The Cross Border Initiative

B: We were awake early on Monday. This was the first day on which our schedule did not include a visit to Zamtan. We were more than a little nervous about what the day ahead might hold. But first we had the luxury of sitting in the back of the car and letting the world pass us by.

Driving to the Kasumbalesa border which separates Zambia from the Congo, crammed into a World Vision vehicle with Fordson, Peter and Jim, gave us an hour or two to fill ourselves in with some facts about the project we were visiting. As far as we have been able to decipher the notes that we scribbled that morning, elbowing each other repeatedly in the process as we balanced our notebooks precariously on our laps, this is what we learned from Fordson.

The Cross Border Initiative, as it was called to start with, began in Tanzania in 1992, on the border between Tanzania and Zambia. In 1996 the Zambian government took up the idea. Its aim was to tackle what has become globally recognized as a vital factor in the fight against AIDS throughout the world: raising awareness about safe sex between sex workers and their clients, the truckers who travel thousands of miles across one African country after another. Border towns in Zambia are busy places. They heave with truckers, traders and a mobile, migrant population attracted by the possibility of making money. Forced to wait at every border for papers to be processed, the truckers are often more than happy to pay for the services of girls propelled by poverty into prostitution.

As soon we begin to visualize the sheer size of the continent of Africa, the number of small countries, and especially the number of those that are landlocked, it is easy to understand how the virus has spread so vigorously. Zambia alone borders nine different countries, each with its own culture, taboos and language. One fact that appeared on just about every item of literature that we were sent before our trip stated that, on average, one out of four people will contract HIV after having sex with an infected person. Bearing that statistic in mind, I try to work something out in my notebook. My maths has never been that good, but I can try.

The loneliness of the long-distance lorry driver

A long-distance lorry driver sets out from Uganda with a cargo bound for South Africa. He will have to cross six countries and stop at twelve border crossings. He will be stuck at each of these borders for up to three weeks. There he may have sex with a girl a night, but let us assume he is more circumspect or short of money and only has sex with a girl every third night. That is 84 girls. If it is every night it would be 252 girls. Any one of those girls might be HIV-positive. When you bear in mind that he has to retrace his entire route in order to get back home (now we are up to at least 168 girls), you realize this means that our driver would have to be incredibly fortunate to escape infection. He will then pass on the infection, and each girl he infects will in turn pass it on to a quarter of her clients.

Now the statistics become truly frightening.

According to the one-in-four statistic, we could now have 42 sex workers who have caught HIV/AIDS from this one man. Most of them will have sex with three or four men per night. Suppose it were only two. Bearing in mind that there are no holidays built into the trucking occupation, each of these 42 sex workers could have intercourse with 730 men a year. Let us take off a few nights for sick leave and nights out with the girls or the boyfriend and take a conservative stab at 700 men each.

700 men times 42 sex workers = 29,400.

Divide this number by four, and there is a very real possibility that 7,350 men could contract HIV/AIDS as a direct consequence of the actions of one lorry driver.

If only it finished here. Each of those men, in their turn, will have sex with – how many girls did I conservatively estimate it to be just now – 168? And they in their turn?

This is how corridors of death have come to be built all over this beautiful continent.

I close my notebook and sit in stunned silence for a few minutes, trying to absorb the horror of the situation. I haven't even mentioned what is perhaps the saddest casualty statistic of all. Most of these truckers will have wives to whom they return at last and there will be great rejoicing. That night he will curl up in bed with his wife and very likely give her a homecoming present of HIV/AIDS. She may also become pregnant. There is a one in four chance that the child will be HIV-positive. He or she will grow up and …

And that is how innumerable little innocent country villages have come to be dying throughout sub-Saharan Africa.

Fordson explained how research demonstrated that there really was only one way to bring about the sort of behavioural change necessary to slow the progress of the pandemic. Dedicated workers needed to get alongside the truckers and the sex workers and, quite simply, *tell them*.

A mission impossible?

It may seem so, but it is worth bearing in mind that similar methods have proved successful in the past. Over two thousand years ago, in fact. When the Son of God was here, he chose just that method to change the world. Take a few dedicated workers, inspire and support them, then get them talking to people everywhere.

It was decided that they should begin by targeting the sex workers, because it was more difficult to build relationships with truckers who were always on the move. A network of houses, all painted blue, was set up to offer support and health care for these women and girls. The charity Society for Family Health provided condoms. US Agency for Internal Development and the Japanese government's Japan International Cooperation Agency provided the funds. But who would provide the vitally important workers who, in partnership with the government and any agency willing to help, could actually make the project work? This, Fordson told us, was where World Vision entered the equation.

When the project started World Vision offered their premises to be used as free drop-in centres. They committed themselves to creating a stigma-free environment, to running programmes designed to both attract clients and bring about behavioural change, and they provided folk who could get alongside both sex workers and truckers. They were able to do a great deal more – according to whatever was needed at the time, in fact. They gave assistance when stocks of medicines ran low, and set up clinics so that blood could be tested right then and there. Basically they were getting on board a vehicle for change that they believed would make a difference. And we were to witness the outcome of these initiatives that day.

On the road

Our journey also gave us a chance to experience driving in Zambia. I had no idea if the road north was typical, but in itself it was very civilized indeed. Not too much traffic. A beautifully smooth, wide, well-maintained road. But the edges finished abruptly, with a sharp drop from the tarmac over a steep ridge to the shrub, with winding dirt tracks leading off to villages as primitive and struggling as Zamtan. This road reflects, perhaps, the position the country has reached in terms of its economy. There is investment and consequent modernization, but it is limited both in monetary amount and in location. Foreign businesses such as those owned by the Japanese government want thriving towns and a good road system that will increase their chances of success. Unproductive villages are hardly worth a second glance, so why bother to invest in roads leading to them? A waste of money.

As I have said, there are not too many cars on Zambia's roads. Few people can afford to drive. Petrol is very expensive. In Zamtan I don't think we met anyone who earned enough to own or drive a vehicle.

Many of the cars we saw were old but appeared to be in a reasonable state. Fordson assured us that the equivalent of our MOT is required annually for every vehicle. Which was why it was such a shock when we passed a local driving instructor and his pupil. The car was made up of patches of red metal which appeared to be held together with even larger patches of rust. The bonnet was battered, the sides were dented, and it looked like an old banger on its way home from a particularly stressful stock-car race. The only thing not falling to pieces was the shiny sign adorning its roof: 'Jerry's Driving School'. What sort of driving instructor is so inept that his car ends up as wrecked as this? What sort of optimistic maniacs are these learner drivers? We had to ask.

"He is cheap. The pupils who pay a lot have a good car to learn on. Jerry has many students, but he is a bad instructor. His pupils keep bumping into things."

So, no dual controls in Jerry's car, then. Maybe no brakes either, judging by the extent of the damage. Apart from anything else, there are very few other cars to bump into. Our minds boggled!

We laughed at the idea of Jerry's Driving School, but there was nothing funny about our frequent encounters with the police at the many checkpoints along that same road. They are a source of much annoyance to locals. Why are the police not out chasing criminals instead of harassing motorists? That was the question we heard on several occasions. Sound familiar?

Dressed in their huge hats, khaki trousers, blue jumpers and white shirts the policemen look quite impressive. But that, we gathered, is nothing compared to the way such a smart uniform makes them feel. They have power, and they love using it. We learned that their zeal is fuelled by the fact that any money they take in fines goes into their own pockets. Just a week before our visit, a member of a World Vision film crew had only escaped prison, or confiscation of his camera, or at the very least a hefty fine, because he was in the company of local World Vision workers who could vouch for him.

We heard another story that illustrated the contempt with which locals view the police and their role. The police stopped a car containing too many passengers, but the passengers all wailed and wept so convincingly, pretending they were on their way to a funeral, that they were allowed to go on their way. However, one policeman was suspicious and followed them on his motorbike. But that big old hat was a giveaway. By the time he drew alongside the car, the passengers had stopped wallowing in their success and returned to their sobbing and wailing. The driver even challenged the policeman over his insensitivity for once more interrupting the funeral party. At which point – and this is why the story has become a legend – the policeman apologized and left hurriedly.

The Drop-in Centre

We were so happy listening to Fordson's stories that we hardly noticed when we turned off the main road to drive through a pleasant residential area. We turned down a side road and pulled up into a driveway. We had arrived. Whatever I was expecting the Chililabombwe Drop-in

Centre to be, it was not this low attractive building with a privet-hedged garden. Nor did I expect the laughter coming from what looked like a small lounge. Nor the sound of drumming from outside, where some young people could be glimpsed dancing on the lawn while others swung on a huge chair swing. Nor the group of young men playing pool in a shed outside. The only thing that did not surprise us was the warmth with which Patrick, the site manager, and his team greeted us. We were getting used to the kindness of Zambians.

We met and joggled for space in what we were informed laughingly was actually Patrick's office, but was used by all, all the time, for everything.

"Oh, yes!" agreed Patrick with a smile.

It was there, crammed in with Patrick, Richard Kapui (manager of planning), Rosa (in charge of funds), Jim, Peter, Fordson and some members of staff to whom we had not yet been introduced, drinking mugs of very welcome coffee, that we learned about the challenges connected with the Centre and its work.

"In a few minutes the wheels of the project will be here, but first I'd like you to meet Violet, who heads up Behavioural Change."

Adrian and I were so used to not having a clue what anyone was talking about that we allowed the above statement to pass without comment and simply asked Violet exactly what her job entailed.

"What you have to understand is that we are constantly breaking new ground, especially with the truckers. Because they are constantly on the move we see different men coming in here all the time. But we are beginning to get excited by what is happening. There is definitely an increase in understanding of the issues involved, and the fact that truckers and sex workers can literally drop into somewhere local means we are seeing a real increase in the numbers coming for testing and counselling. And now that we've got our own clinic we're able to store the drugs to treat infections on the spot now. We're running some pretty dynamic programmes which you are going to see later to attract the sex workers, and these are proving really successful.

"It sounds as if it's all going really well," I said enthusiastically.

There was a pause.

"It is going well. But it's such a huge challenge. There is no room for complacency. We've got some trucking companies responding positively, but others are completely against the whole thing. Those who come from countries where all men are circumcised soon after birth, and therefore cannot contract STIs (sexually transmitted infections), tend to be less interested. Then, you know, we have problems with libel laws. How do you convince truckers of their responsibility for the spread of AIDS without actually accusing them? What we're trying to do is never easy."

The joy of winning

Fordson the footballer (centre, green shirt)

Rodrick with his wife outside their shop

A whirling welcome to church

The still centre

A rare moment of relaxation

Chililabombwe drama group

Chilufya

Sex worker, netball player and full-time mum

A football team of sex workers

Auntie Doris at the border with a truck driver

Girls in the compound

A peer educator working with two 'queen mothers'

Philemon shows how it's done

Adrian counting money outside Rodrick's shop

Hope for the future – the Sanduka girls with staff from the training centre

"What about the girls?"

"The sex workers? Complicated again." Violet looked rueful. "I'll let the peer educators tell you about that. Are they here, Patrick?"

"They're waiting to meet you. It's getting a bit squashed in here! I tell you what, let's have a tour around the building and then you may find you have some more questions for them."

Posters

A: We set off on our tour.

Exploring buildings can be a groaningly tedious business. Rooms are just rooms until something is happening in them. It is rather different here, partly because of the infectious creative energy of the people who are showing us round, and partly because there is something about the Drop-in Centre itself. An atmosphere of warmth, urgency and developing confidence has embraced and involved Bridget and me from the moment we arrived.

As we move around the Centre we become aware of colourful posters on the walls of corridors and offices, all in English for some reason, and almost exclusively to do with the fight against AIDS.

'Free your mind from worries about HIV' says one, the words printed across the forehead and, like a necklace, under the chin of a happily smiling man. Another version of the same poster features a beautiful young woman.

Another poster is for established couples and married people. A man and a woman are pictured cuddled together, clearly in love. This time the message is 'Where there is love, use it!'. The legend is situated directly beside a packet of condoms.

Yet another poster pictures an older man talking to two young friends at the corner of a pool table, his arms around their shoulders. 'Tell your friends that trust alone is not enough' urges this poster issued by an organization called HEART (Helping Each Other Act Responsibly Together).

Another HEART production is very pink, presumably to appeal to pre- and early-teen girls. Since having a daughter of my own I have been forced to seriously take on board the awesome fact that pink is the universal colour of choice for girls in this age range. The four girls pictured here, pretty and colourfully dressed, one clutching a fluffy toy, are twinkling examples of those youngsters who fall within the age parameters of the Window of Hope initiative. They smile confidently into the camera. 'Not everyone is doing it, we are NOT!' they declare in the caption at the top of the picture and, at the bottom, 'Virgin Power – Virgin Pride'.

'No condom no sex' the next poster bluntly advises those who have passed beyond or away from this stage in their lives and outlook. 'Don't take chances – use a condom every time you have sex'.

The message is everywhere. It is not subtle, but I find myself wondering how many times yet another sad, lingering death has been avoided because one person passing through this building has just happened to become aware, literally, of the writing on the wall.

Condoms

In the course of our tour we arrive at a small office and peer through the door. My attention is immediately caught by one of the shelves in this room that is groaning beneath the weight of a vast pile of boxes. They all contain condoms. Hundreds of condoms. Probably thousands of condoms. All made by a firm called 'MAXIMUM'.

Coming from a culture where the rude mechanics of birth control are not exactly a common topic of discussion, it suddenly feels very strange and, if I am honest, a trifle uncomfortable, to find myself in a world where posters and broadcasts and conversations and office shelves are awash with condoms. I recall how, as a young teenager who looked older than his age, I was always deeply puzzled by the question that my local hairdresser inexplicably asked after the final snip of a monthly haircut had been executed, and the naked flame of a lighted taper had been passed with pungent effect across the hair ends at the nape of my neck.

"Anything for the weekend, sir?"

What, I used to ask myself with a bewildered shake of the head on these occasions, could this man possibly have for sale that he thinks I would be likely to need at the weekend? What sort of thing do you need at the weekend? And why on earth does he find it necessary to ask his peculiar question in such a significantly weighted, discreet tone of voice?

Even now, after all the years that have passed, I feel my toes curl with embarrassment as I picture my younger self gazing with perplexity at plastic combs, jars of oily hair cream, small mirrors and bottles of watery shampoo before brightly replying that I was sure I had 'enough of everything I need until next month, thank you very much for asking'.

I suppose I was a naïve lad.

I tell myself to face facts. I find the whole thing nightmarish and slightly nauseous, but I know full well that, like many other similarly affected countries, Zambia desperately needs to be awash with condoms. I pray to God that all the work being done with schoolchildren and young people will result increasingly in abstinence as the preferred means of avoiding infection and unwanted pregnancy, but in the meantime babies are being conceived and born. Children are being orphaned. The evil tide has to be halted, or at least slowed. Canute-like moral stances conducted on lofty parts of the beach that the sea never reaches are of no use to anyone. When the Son of God dances he doesn't mind getting his feet wet from time to time. He never did, thank goodness.

Outreach

We move on to the Outreach Room, equipped with comfortable chairs and a large television attached to a video player. This is a place where truck drivers (the group from which most of the sex workers' clients are drawn), sex workers themselves, young people and anyone else who is concerned or interested can watch educational videos, discuss relevant issues with a counsellor and take advantage of free distribution of a few of those thousands of condoms that are kept on the office shelves.

"Funny thought," I whisper to Bridget, "that truck drivers sit in here watching videos about truck drivers and sex workers. Do you think they have a problem realizing that it's all about them at first?"

Bridget nods. "Yes, I should imagine they probably wake up with a sort of shock when they understand just how important their decisions might be. I mean, whatever happens that same night really could be a matter of life or death, couldn't it?"

Absolutely right, and I shudder as I consider that, as Bridget had already concluded after her scribbled calculations in the car, this is one of the most deeply frightening aspects of a pandemic like AIDS. Every single individual decision about abstinence or the wearing of a condom could potentially affect the lives of many, many people for better or for worse. Earlier in the week my own sensibilities had been confused and over-whelmed by the experience of witnessing hundreds of schoolchildren performing sketches, poems and songs, some of them quite explicit, about the dangers of HIV/AIDS. Why did it trouble me so much? I suppose it was just that, from my British, middle-class perspective, there was an aura of dank tastelessness around the notion that children should have their minds filled with such grotesquely gloomy images at such an early age. Now, as I stand at the door of this room and think seriously about the far-reaching consequences of one solitary right or wrong decision, I am glad. Let all the children be prepared. Let those often-repeated words of warning echo around their minds as they grow older, and let it give them pause when serious choices have to be made. Let them live.

Treatment

The Treatment Room is an important and highly valued part of the Drop-in Centre – especially in recent times, we gather, as the health department now supplies a trained nurse to work with patients who need screening or testing or treatment. In the old days a client would have to wait up to three months for the results of his or her test to be sent back to the Centre. Patrick tells us that many of the men and women involved find it hard enough to present themselves for testing in the first place. It is all too easy for shyness and fear to drown out the voice of common sense. In the past, patients would quite often fail to turn up for that second crucial appointment after three months had passed, which meant that someone would have to make the attempt to track them down and persuade them to return to the Drop-in Centre. Now that a nurse is on the team most things can be done on the spot, and this contraction of the process in terms of time has obvious benefits. In three months an awful lot of people can be infected and, in their turn, pass infection on to others.

Counselling

Kavwumba Maluwa is a warm, motherly person possessed of the immediately evident, virtually indefinable gift that is sometimes called stillness. I have known and valued people like Kavwumba in the past. Her persona is a peaceful pool into which anything and everything may be thrown. Things that need never be seen again can quietly sink and disappear. Those things that must be looked at will bob and float gently on the surface of her attention, made amazingly harmless for a just a little while, because she will not allow them to create destructive waves.

We discover her in the Counselling Room, a small, darkened area, simply furnished with a table and two or three easy chairs. From a pale coloured wall opposite the door one of those 'Free Your Mind' posters promises confidential testing and counselling. It is the second part of this promise that Kavwumba is responsible for keeping. She is crucial to each phase of a client's involvement with the Centre, offering counselling before and after testing. Coaxing, encouragement and information are needed at every stage of what can be a very frightening process.

"It is common," Kavwumba tells us, "for my clients to be in crisis, either because they are worried that they might have AIDS, or because they are terrified to hear the results of their test. They can become very emotional. Some people know deep down from the beginning that they have the virus, but it is still a huge shock to find out for sure. I try to prepare them as well as I can for the bad things that they have to hear."

"What are some of the things that help you in doing that?" someone asks, perhaps assuming that Kavwumba will list one or two advanced counselling techniques that she regularly employs.

Her reply brings a smile to my face.

"Tea is good," she says.

That is advanced enough for me, I reflect. If I was faced with hearing really bad news, I would prefer it to happen in the presence of Kavwumba Maluwa and a cup of tea.

"It is not an easy job," she continues. "I see maybe five or six clients each day, and when the strain begins to tell on me I cannot pass it on to them, so I need to have the opportunity to ventilate my feelings with colleagues and peers. If I could not do that it would be too difficult."

We thank Maluwa for her time and turn to leave. As we start to file out I become vaguely aware that there is another woman in the room, sitting in the shadowed space behind the door. I barely register her existence, and then we are gone.

Embarrassing tee shirts

B: Back in Patrick's office for the second time, we were even cosier. Veronica, Bridget, Charity, Ackim and Steven, five of the project's peer educators and, as Patrick now reiterated, 'the wheels of the project', now joined us.

"Talk to us about the girls," was Adrian's direct request.

"Where do we start?"

"How about at the beginning? How do they get into this?"

I could hear the agitation in Steven's voice and guessed he was struggling with it as much as I was.

"Well, from all our surveys and from speaking to those we meet, one thing is clear. The current reality for these young women is very different from the dreams and ambitions they had as children. Most of them went to church. Went to school. Most of them dropped out of school because one or both parents died. Not all – of course some of the girls got pregnant while they were at school, and some of them dropped out because they hated it. But the huge majority of them are orphans. They drifted to the borders because they were hungry and the border towns have a reputation for being places where you can make a living somehow. A lot of the girls begin by selling stuff – bananas, potatoes, that sort of thing. But the stark truth is that there is more regular money to be made from sex work. You know you will eat today. It's food security."

Those words again. Food security. Never before had I understood so clearly that the devil can use hunger and poverty as tools.

"What sort of ages are we talking about?"

"Most of them are under sixteen when they start. Schoolgirls. Some of them are as young as eleven."

"You can usually pick them out – the new ones," chipped in Charity. "Not just by their age but by the way they look. Shy, badly dressed, scared, obviously in-experienced. The saddest thing about this work is that we witness how they change. Become hardened, tougher, skilled at handling men and negotiating their fee. They are difficult to reach then. We are trying to get to them before they get to that stage. While behavioural change is still possible. Before they have children. Before they get sick."

I looked across at Adrian and heard his unspoken "Before they die" as loudly as if he had shouted it.

What Charity said reminded me of teenage girls I had worked with in the UK who had had to survive horrific circumstances and who had become emotionally bruised and damaged in the process. Young women have a very complicated and delicately balanced hormonal equilibrium which can swing way off balance if things happen to radically disturb it. Often, unable to cope deep down with what has happened to them, they become hardened and unreachable.

I wanted to move the discussion on.

"So, what are your greatest challenges?"

"Apart from coming to terms with wearing these tee shirts?"

This comment brought shared laughter. Pictures of truckers and girls emblazoned on your front and the Corridors of Hope logo on the back is hardly subtle, but they know they need to establish exactly who they are before they even introduce themselves.

"I suppose for me it's the constant adjustment – I mean, the girls who come here can be anything from twelve to thirty, so we have to find activities tailored to their age."

"We have to get used to being rejected. Not everyone wants to hear what we have to say, you know."

"Then there's the frustration. You meet them. You get on really well. You set up a meeting here. And they don't come."

"Or they come drunk. Or you see they've got drugs. Yes, that's it for me too."

"There is a big challenge for the men. I would be telling lies if I said this work does not have its temptations, because if we help the girls they might offer us free sex as a way of saying thank you. We try to use this as a chance to tell them of the dangers, but sometimes they are insulted. They say that we will know where to find them if we have a change of heart. But we must be strong. If we sample a client it will destroy the trust we have built that there is a different and safer way to live. We must remain true to our calling. But it is a big challenge."

"I think for me it's feeling pretty useless. Sometimes they say, 'Offer me an alternative and I'll stop.' What can you say? It's no good giving them money. They need something a lot more. Of course, we've got Sanduka now."

Sanduka?

Letter

A: Before we had time to discover exactly what Sanduka might mean, Patrick came into the room carrying a sheet of paper and squeezed through to the photocopier. He looked excited.

"This is what makes what we are doing worthwhile. I've just had a letter from a girl who wants to stop what she's doing. I think she means it, too. You know sometimes they say they do and two days later change their minds. But this one – I'm pretty sure she means it."

"Can we see the letter?"

"Don't see why not. She said she didn't mind who I showed it to if it meant she got a job."

This is the letter that Patrick handed to us:

THE MANAGER,
WORLD VISION
CHILILABOMBWE
16.07.2004

Dear Sir / Madam

RE: ASSISTANCE FROM YOUR ORGANIZATION

I am a young lady aged 24 yrs old wishing to stop operating as a sex worker, knowing my HIV status. I completed my O Levels as well as my college in Uganda Kampala where I obtained a Diploma in Tourism and Travel (TATA UFTAA

COURSES) and a certificate in computers. Due to lack of employment and lack of parents to support my everyday life I decided to join the sex workers.

I am very much concerned about my life and my future and my young brother who I am taking care of. I therefore humbly request your caring organization to offer me assistance in terms of employment to enable me to lead a satisfying life.

I will highly appreciate your positive response towards my application.

Yours faithfully

Chilufya Mwila

"Did it come in the post?" Adrian leaned forward.

"No, she brought it in herself this morning." Patrick rises briskly to his feet. "I think she's here now. Look, if you don't mind I think we'd better move on. Judging by the volume of the drums outside I think our drama group is ready to show you something. It's one of our programmes that has a double purpose. It attracts outsiders to come in and it's helping to find an alternative occupation for a couple of our girls who've made the decision to stop sex working. I think you'll be impressed."

The drama group

B: 'You can touch my body
You can touch my breasts
But not my private parts
You cannot have sex with me …'

As song choruses go this one is nothing if not memorable. But then, that is the aim.

The members of the Chililabombwe drama and singing group are committed to one thing. They want to get across the stark message that it is very, very important to be careful about the way you enter into and conduct relationships. If you do not take this care you might become infected.

The fact that the group is made up of two young women who have been sex workers at the border crossing and four young men who have been involved in 'unhelpful lifestyles' add to the power of what they are trying to convey.

And convey it they do.

Mind you, before they began they had displayed considerable nervousness. They had fidgeted and shuffled, straightened caps, tightened scarves round their waists and fussed with their hair. They were clearly a group of young, inexperienced amateurs. They were about to perform in front of a group of total strangers including a cameraman and a photographer, so I didn't blame them one bit for finding the situation daunting. There was nothing atmospheric about dancing on a patch of grass outside a Drop-in Centre, and we were only standing a few feet away from them.

But from the moment the drum started to beat we knew we were about to see something special. Moving in unison, they followed their lead singer as he stepped into the centre and set the pace, punching the air rhythmically with his fist.

'Neata neatata
Neata neatata
Oh la leiey
Oh la leiey'

His voice charged with alarm and tension, he began slowly.

'RISE ... Rise from the jungle
Be aware
Be awaey aware'

Crouching down in a semicircle, they then straightened up slowly, arms outstretched with palms extended upwards.

'RISE ... Rise from the jungle
Be aware
Be awaey aware'

The leader dramatically pointed to the corner, shouting out his next words in a voice that was filled with terror.

'What can I see coming from over there?'

The backing group shaded their eyes with their hands and peered enthusiastically around.

'Where? Where? Where?'

We never found out what they actually saw, as English was abandoned at that point, but I suspect it was HIV/AIDS which was lurking unseen.

The drama built with variations of tempo and movements and, watching and listening closely, we became aware that the chorus cropped up frequently. Each time they sang the chorus one of the girls would move into the centre with one of the men facing her front and the other facing her back. The human sandwich then moved as one, accompanied by a rhythmic drum beat. The first time they did this I admit we were a bit shocked. It was very graphic. But, as each time the movements were absolutely identical, it soon became clear that this was not sleazy 'dirty dancing' but a carefully choreographed piece of theatre. The sex act itself was almost mechanically displayed by energetic pelvic thrusting on the part of both young men, accentuated by the vigorously moving tassels on the scarves round their waists. The fact that there was no eye contact, combined with the clinical lack of emotion, created a strangely disturbing atmosphere. I realized that they were simply putting the actions to the words with no more or less emotional involvement than when they had shaded their eyes earlier. We needed to know what the words meant. The stark, simple message about breasts, bodies and private parts was translated for us by one of the facilitators who was standing proudly with us in order to explain what we were seeing.

Both of the girls were superb natural dancers. One of the youths had an exceptional talent for acting. He looked good, thin and edgy, baseball cap on back to front, tee shirt and jeans carrying gothic logos, but the thing that made him stand out was his extraordinarily mobile face.

He really came into his own during the second song, which followed seamlessly on from the first, the bridge created by gunshots of words accompanying the increasingly frenetic drumming.

'Neata neatata
Neata neatata
Oh la leiey
Oh la leiey'

Head thrown back, he swaggered into the centre and then proceeded to mime laughing, dancing, partying and drinking before transforming himself into a staggering drunk who wept, then coughed and died. And all this with the confidence and skill of an experienced actor. The words, thankfully in English, were belted out by the rest of the group with a great deal of energy but perhaps rather too much enjoyment. They had relaxed and were having a great time as they sang the following words repeatedly with interludes of drumming breaking it up while the principal actor showed what he could do.

'One day I met a lady
She called herself Maria
One day I met a lady
She called herself Maria
Oh poor me
My baby was a liar
Why can't you try and lose her?
My baby was a liar
And when my body's wasted
My baby is delighted
Poor me'

Their dance ended and they gathered in a group to receive their ovation. Then the girls wandered over to the seat swing and talked quietly to each other. The lads dispersed, probably back to a well-earned game of pool. Adrian disappeared as well, and I had a few minutes to reflect on what had just bombarded my senses.

Two things struck me. These young people were comfortable with their sexuality. I later read a quotation from American writer Don Schrader that reinforced my first impression. In response to the traditional Christian insistence on separating sex from spirituality he wrote, 'To hear many religious people talk, one would think God created the torso, head, legs and arms, but the devil slapped on the genitalia.'

Here there was no shame attached to the enactment of the sexual act. It came across as no more significant than any of the other actions in the song. The dance was not intended to titillate or shock us. There were no sideways glances to gauge the reactions of respectable middle-aged foreigners to their performance. No defiance of possible censure. They were proud of their production as theatre and also as propaganda. In language designed for their peer group, the message was crystal clear.

'You are young. You will want to have physical contact. This is as much a practical issue as a moral one. To stay alive you can touch, but that is as far as you can go.'

The other thing that struck me was my own sincere relief that these six young people were no longer at immediate risk. All of them were earning a little money from their performances and had regular contact with the peer educators as they planned new performance pieces. There was a structure to prevent them from returning to their past way of life, and they had hope for the future. Angela, bubbly, strong and confident, was not going to waste away slowly. Her chrysanthemum bloom of springy burgundy-tinted hair would not be reduced to lifeless straggles. Her robust body would not rot with any of the opportunist diseases which would otherwise eventually have killed her. The permanently troubled expression on Heather's pretty face suggested that her past had left deep scars, but she too had gained many extra years of life in which healing could take place. The lads would play pool and sing and drum and find jobs and not die – at least not yet. They may all live to a good old age. At least they have a chance now, and through the message they communicate they are working to give others that chance. Thank God for Corridors of Hope.

The girl in the corner

A: "She's here now."

Those were the words that Patrick said immediately before we left the office a few minutes ago. I remember now. Of course those were the words. So, in that case . . .

When it comes to making connections, I think my mind must be a little strange. It surprises and confuses people sometimes. I can, for instance, quite easily make the connection between bouncy castles and the kingdom of God. How could anyone not? And it seems odd to me that everyone is not immediately aware of what we can learn about transfiguration from watching two young people carry an old table on to a train. A roadside skip offers the most transparent parable of forgiveness that it is possible to imagine, and what could present a clearer picture of the need for passion in the church than a breakage in the pickle aisle of a local supermarket? These pairings and parallels are the easy, obvious ones as far as I am concerned. My difficulty comes when what most other people would call a normal, logical connection happens right in front of my nose. For a long time I just don't register it. Then, suddenly, I make the connection.

This is what is happening now at Chililabombwe, as we stand outside the Drop-in Centre watching two startlingly vivid pieces of drama being presented by six talented young people. It is just as their second performance ends, and I have begun to applaud with genuine appreciation, that the penny drops. It is in connection with the letter we were shown in the office a little earlier, the one from the girl who has written to World Vision asking for a job. The words on that sheet of paper moved me deeply. Why? I think because it was so painfully clear that the young woman who wrote them had folded her yearning, panic-stricken plea so inadequately, and with such hopeful care, into the flimsy wrapping of a formal approach. It must be the equivalent of filling in an application form to be rescued from a shark.

Patrick made a brief comment about this girl immediately after standing up. It was just a few words, and now I have remembered what he said. The girl is here, he told us. She is here. She is actually present in the Centre. In that case – in that case the person I fleetingly noticed, sitting so nervously behind the door in the corner of the Counselling Room as we passed through in the course of our tour – that must have been her. The girl who wrote the letter was in that dark little room. I try hard to remember her face or the clothes she was wearing, but my mind is a blank. I threw only the briefest of glances at the girl in the corner as I left. She could have been a member of the staff for all I knew.

Suddenly, in my heart, I know that I want to see her and, if possible, speak to her. As usual, our benevolent juggernaut of a programme is preparing to roll itself and us on to the next stage of the itinerary, but it's no good. I want to talk to the person who wrote that letter. The rest will just have to wait. Without saying anything, even to Bridget, I turn and head for the door of the Drop-in Centre.

Access to beauty

Back inside the building I knock gently on the door of the Counselling Room and hear Kavwumba Maluwa's comfortable voice on the other side inviting me to come in. Entering, I allow myself one quick glance to confirm that the girl in the corner is still there. Yes, I do remember enough to know that the girl who is sitting there now is the same one who was there before.

Mrs Maluwa tells me that she is in the middle of a counselling session. I apologize for interrupting and explain that Patrick has shown us the letter that her client wrote to the Centre. It is a great intrusion, but could she possibly ask the young lady if she would be kind enough to answer some questions about her life and her hopes for the future?

I am not sure if she really approves but, smiling and nodding, the counsellor turns and addresses the person who is sitting, so still and so fragile, in the seat opposite her. As she speaks I perch on the edge of the table and look properly at the girl in the corner for the first time.

She is a true beauty, this woman. The eyes beneath her dark, cropped hair are large and lustrous, her mouth wide and generous, the expression on her exquisitely-shaped face one of intelligence and deep unhappiness. She is wearing jeans and a black jumper over her slight, almost boyish figure and two thin gold-coloured chains around her neck. Her frame is perfect but tiny in construction. I suspect that her body appears more delicately fragile than it should because proper nourishment has been lacking from her diet. An entirely natural sophisticate, there is no apparent trace of flamboyancy or cheapness in this girl – this sex worker.

A question for myself. Why is it disturbing me so much to see her sitting here looking so trim and troubled and so very attractive? It is certainly not simply that I sympathize with her plight although, of course, I do. That is what has drawn me back to this room. My disturbance stems from something less comfortable and more complicated than that. Perhaps it is to do with an unaccustomed and awkward dislodgement of the male psyche that is almost bound to occur in a situation like this. People like us, in books like the one you are reading now, tend to write about issues involving sex workers as though there is no complexity or entanglement in our response to such people and such issues. In fact, of course, all such encounters pass through the filter of what we were and are and hope to become. In the light and shadow of that reality we may discover a little more of the truth.

I suddenly recall a moment in one of those mega-popular American sitcoms. A man confesses to his fiancée that he has been flirting with the pizza-delivery girl.

She smiles and says that he mustn't worry about such a small thing.

He is relieved and impressed. Wow! Mustn't worry. What a woman!

Goodness, no, she continues, flirting means nothing. Everyone does it. She does it all the time herself.

Suddenly he is very upset. She does it all the time? He had thought it was just men who did that sort of thing.

She is puzzled. Why does it matter so much?

Now he becomes a little wild. She clearly doesn't understand a man's point of view, he says. When a girl is even mildly flirtatious with a man, all he can think about is whether or not she wants to have sex with him. So do women feel that way as well, he asks frantically? He had thought it was only men whose minds worked like that! Does her mind work like that?

That character is right, of course – about men, I mean – I have no idea if it applies to women as well. He may be overstating the case a little, but it is true (I understand from others less pure than myself) that even the most saintly examples of the male species have a tendency, however fleeting, to automatically assess the women they meet in terms of sexual attraction and accessibility. Having said that, they – oh, all right, we – don't necessarily assent to or approve of this undistinguished little mechanism in ourselves. It just happens. More often than not, especially for those of us who genuinely believe in the dignity and value of each person that we meet, it is recognized as a physiologically based nuisance that just has to be set aside, and certainly not entertained or indulged.

For me, as for many, that was certainly not always the case. As a young man I took a rabid interest in all young females, mentally indulging and entertaining like mad. Being a seriously uncool and rather plain youth (it was to be several years before my looks started to become 'interesting'), most of my entertaining and indulging was confined to the inside of my head. Nevertheless, I continued to, as it were, stack the girls I met into whichever of my private categories applied to them.

Too old to have sex with. Too young to have sex with. Too experienced and therefore too frightening to have sex with. Too rich to be interested in having sex with someone as impoverished as me. Too pretty to ever contemplate having sex with anyone as unprepossessing as me. Smiled at me once, so might remotely toy with the possibility of having sex with me. Smiled at me twice so might really consider having sex with me. Talked and listened to me as if I were a human being, so might be interested in having sex with my personality, if you know what I mean (which would be more than fine). Too strikingly, blindingly beautiful to ever have sex with anyone as insignificant as me because she could have the choice of absolutely anyone she wanted.

Yes, there were indeed girls who were so beautiful, and therefore so remotely inaccessible, that I was obliged to place them firmly, instantly and forever into the 'never will be available' category. This is all very silly and shallow, a part of growing up, and in any case I know now that affection and friendship were what I was really looking for, but it does, I think, offer a clue to the reason for my acute discomfort as I gaze at the beautiful girl in the chair opposite.

Unless you are one of the fortunate, tiny minority that are solvent, beauty is a very limited currency in countries like Zambia. In rich countries such as ours, rightly or wrongly, exceptionally good looks allow choice in relationships and can confer a sort of social celebrity on those who are fortunate enough to possess them. For Zambian women like this one, penniless and alone, there is only one way in which such looks can be cashed in or marketed, and that is through the sex trade.

I or anyone else could buy this girl for £1 if we wanted. And that, I now realize, is the root of my profound uneasiness. If I really, really wanted I could buy access to all that exquisite delicacy and beauty using a fraction of the spare cash that I have in my back pocket at this moment. For the equivalent of £5 I could probably own her for a week, and she would do anything I asked.

I don't like it. I loathe it. It is sickeningly wrong. All wrong. All screwed-up and obscene and wrong. Like so many of the dankly unnatural short cuts that are offered to us by the devil, this one takes truth and rightness and turns them, not on their heads – because that would produce paradoxes and paradoxes are gloriously useful – but into ghastly, truncated, twisted versions of themselves. I hate it.

Thank God that this girl is seeking a way out. The Son of God has begun to dance in her life, and with the help of Kavwumba Maluwa and others at the Centre, the devil will have no choice but to retreat.

She agrees to talk to me, and to Bridget, who has now arrived in the room looking for me. I know from the signature on her letter that the girl's name is Chilufya. We ask her to tell us about her life. She leans forward to speak, hope and intensity contained and brimming up to the very edge of herself like the contents of an overfilled glass. Her voice is soft and tentative. This is her story.

Chilufya's story

"I had quite a good start in life, better than a lot of other children, at any rate. I grew up in the care of my mother and father, attending school, and then college, where I was trained in tourism and travel. It was the kind of career that I believed would really suit me well. My dream was always to one day have a job that would allow me to work with people.

"I was only twenty years old when my father and mother both died within quite a short space of time. I was very, very upset. I had to go with my younger brother Nkaka to stay with relatives in Uganda. But life was no easier for people there than in our home country. Before long I was told that I must go back to Zambia with my brother and look for work. A good thing was that my mother had two sisters living back here in Zambia. My brother and I were allowed to go and live with one of these ladies, but, sadly, the same thing happened as when we lived with our parents. The aunt we were staying with died, and Nkaka and I moved in with my mother's second sister in Lusaka. After seven months this lady quite suddenly told us that we had to leave. It was horrible.

"'I don't like you,' she told us, just like that, 'pack your things. Go and find a job.'

"It was four o'clock in the morning when we were turned out of the house. We had no friends and nowhere to go.

"On the following Wednesday, after a very bad week in the city, there was some good news. It came in the form of a message that was sent by a man who owned shops in the city. The message was, 'If you see Chilufya tell her to come and see me. Her father was from a good family, I will give her an interview.'

"I was so excited! I attended for the interview and was overjoyed to be offered a job. I was to be employed as a cashier in a shop. Things went very well for a month. The shop supervisor told me that I was a good member of staff, and that he liked me very much. He was always complimenting me on my work.

"Then things began to go wrong. One day he came to me and said, 'I want to ask you out.' I refused, but every day he said the same thing. 'I want to take you out.' It got worse. He began to make other demands, things that were even more difficult to accept. Such things as, 'I want to kiss you.'

"I was worried because I had been given a job at last and did not want to lose it. I also feared that if I went on saying 'no' the supervisor might hit me or chase me.

"I had made a few friends in the city by now. I asked their advice. What did they think I should do? They had no doubts at all. I must certainly refuse his advances. I listened to what they said and told the man firmly that I would not do any of the things that he wanted.

"From that moment the supervisor's attitude was completely different. He became cold and distant. He seemed to be always looking for faults in my work, even though I was trying to work as hard and as well as I could. He shouted at me in front of the customers and made me feel stupid. I became more and more nervous and afraid. I decided that if I could find another job I would leave this place that was becoming so unpleasant and difficult to work in. But, though I looked very hard, there were no other jobs to be found, and the supervisor's behaviour was getting even worse. He shouted at me all the time, and told the manager that my work was no good. Often I could hear him laughing at me with other people behind my back.

"At last I said to myself, 'I just cannot stand this any longer. I shall go to see one of my friends in Lusaka and tell her that I want to get another job.'

"So I left my good job in the middle of the month and was allowed to stay in a compound with that friend for a time. But there was no spare money. There never is spare food or money in our country. After a time the friend said that we could not stay there for free. She asked me to pay some money. But there was none.

"'Where do I go now?' I asked myself, 'I must have somewhere for myself and for my brother.'

"I went to another friend's house and she said that I could bring Nkaka to stay there also. It was this friend who introduced me to a different way of making money. If I became a commercial sex worker, she said, I would be able to buy food and pay the rent and look after my brother. I had no choices left any more. I decided to do it.

"But it was never what I wanted. Over and over again as I got involved in this way of making money, I said to myself, 'I know I can't be doing this. I know I can't be doing this!'

"After much worry I decided to take an HIV test. Maybe I was sick. If not, perhaps I could get a job and start a new life. So I took the HIV test. If only my mother had been there. Mum was always advising me what to do. But Mum had died of cancer. I was full of fear as I waited for the results of my test. If I was sick, what would happen to my brother?

"The test was HIV-negative. I was relieved and very surprised. I thanked Jesus for my good fortune. But the doctors said that I should not be too happy too soon. I might still turn out to be positive in three months, when I was due to have the test again.

"I knew that this was the time when I should have changed my life, but I did not. The only change I made for the better was to insist that my clients wear condoms.

"Six months later I had my second test. It was still negative.

"Now," says Chilufya, leaning even further towards us and trembling almost imperceptibly with emotion as she concludes her account, "I have to stop. I can stop. If I am negative six months after the last test I shall know that I am not sick with HIV. It is now three months until that third test. I am negative. I can stop. I can. If I am working I can live my life. I can look after my brother. I am looking for a job – that is why I wrote the letter. I will do whatever job. If I have a job I can get a room for me and my brother in Lusaka and all will be well ..."

Chilufya's journey home

I thank Chilufya for telling me her story and ask if she has a church background. Now she leans back and her gaze drops to the floor.

"Yes," she says in an even softer voice than she has used until now. "I was brought up as a Christian, but I do not attend church now."

"But," I say to her, "if you can get a job and leave the sex work behind, do you think you will go back to church?"

When she finally looks up at me, her dark eyes are wide and luminous.

"How can I go back?" she says, her voice breaking a little. "When I am near a church all I can see are the things I have done. How can God even look at me, knowing what I have been?"

I have felt at a loss many times since arriving in Zambia, but here at least is an opportunity to say something about which I am absolutely certain and clear. My Christian walk over 40 years has left me with many more questions than answers, that is for sure. We deal with answers as small children deal with pets. We put them in a cage and assume they will survive forever, but most of them expire after a fairly short period. At the same time, there are one or two conclusions that seem to have entered into my very bones. They have become the skeleton or framework on which my understanding and awareness of God have been fleshed out and given the support and strength to survive.

Love and obedience, those are two of the most vital structures that uphold us in our relationship with Jesus. The backbone of our faith.

We are drawn by the Father's love and inspired to obedience by the welcome that we receive from him. We shall fail. Yes, we shall. It is inevitable. When that happens we are encouraged to confess our failure and to express our determination to be obedient in the future. God will forgive us for Jesus' sake and because he loves us, even though he knows full well that it will be only a matter of time before we fail once more. But we really will go on trying to be obedient.

To use the apostle Paul's analogy, we will run the race as hard as we can, and when we stumble and fall we will rise quickly to our feet (possibly aided by the helping hand of a friend), dust ourselves off, take a few deep breaths and continue towards the finishing line.

Salvation was entirely the Father's initiative in the first place. His idea. He has made a billion new beginnings available to this world that he loves with such a passion. And Chilufya is a part of that. She is catered for. A grand party is planned for her when she lifts her eyes towards her Father's house and decides to return home.

I do my best to convey these things to her as clearly as I can. I tell her that God always did love her, and that this love has never wavered or changed, regardless of what she has done. I remind her of the prodigal son and tell her what happiness she will bring to the heart of God when she allows him to embrace his troubled daughter once again.

In those dark, frightened eyes of hers I fancy I can see a spark of hope, but perhaps this spark has not yet ignited her will. It is not as easy as all that when you are hungry.

And here's the thing – or one of the things. I suppose, as you read this book, some of you might wonder whether this is a thinly veiled device for raising more money. Well, I think I might remove the veil altogether. Yes, I shall say, you are dead right. We do want to raise more money. We want to raise more money because we have had to sit opposite people like Chilufya Mwila, and we have read in the expressions on their faces a panic-stricken terror that good intentions, however genuine, will not survive the grinding misery of chronic, unrelieved hunger, when a couple of ten-minute sessions in the cab of a lorry each evening will put food on the table and keep a younger brother in school.

Oh, yes, we need to raise more money. You see, our brothers and sisters are in trouble, and many of them want to come home.

The sports teams

B: Reluctantly we left Chilufya to join Patrick for the next stage of our tour. We were, of course, going to be late! But for once I didn't mind. I was seriously jittery. The moment I had been dreading since leaving England had come.

Itinerary: visit – Adrian and Bridget Plass:
Day 6 Item 4: Meet Commercial Sex Workers.

And say what, exactly?

Ask what?

Traditional interview questions were hardly going to fit this particular bill. 'Do you enjoy your job?' would be out, for starters – or would it? Oh, dear, was I the right person to be tackling such a task? I doubted it.

No, I knew who would be perfect for this encounter. A young, cool, liberated, sassy woman who would be completely unfazed when chatting via a translator she had never met before about the pros and cons of condom use in casual sex, who wouldn't worry about blushing or twitching with embarrassment. I was not such a woman. I was going to fail.

Walking along totally absorbed in my thoughts, sternly issuing my own instructions to pull myself together and to stop being such a wimp, I hardly noticed we'd come to a halt until I crashed into Adrian's back. We were in some sort of large sports field which, the sign announced, belonged to Konkola Sports Club. A huge netball and football tournament was in full swing. Judging by the speed, energy and skill that about fifty young women and a few men were displaying, I decided this must be a local sports college.

"They look amazingly good," I commented.

"Oh, they are. Three of these girls play for the Zambian national football team."

Patrick was calling to one of the girls to come and join us. He explained that this was Christabel Mwelwa, who had made the decision to leave her trade as a sex worker and return to school. As she approached us at a run I told myself how wonderful it was to give a girl from such a background the opportunity to join a team of this calibre.

I made a mental note that I needed to get the name of the college before moving on.

Christabel was beautiful. She positively shone with health and self-confidence, and she was more than happy to share her history with us. This is what she told us.

Christabel's story

"I am twenty-two years old. When I was younger my friends told me I was wasting time staying at my home because there was no work. So I went to Konkola. It is a mining town. I met a man and married him and had two children with him, but he was irresponsible and left us. There was never enough to eat. I am not ashamed of my decision to become a sex worker. It was a solution to our poverty. There was somewhere for me and my children to live. But one day I came to the Centre and I was told about the risks. I decided I would like to stop being a sex worker and World Vision attached a worker to me to help me. I wanted to go back to school, but who would help me? At first my support was erratic. Sometimes there was no one to look after my children. The people from the Centre helped me, and now I receive money from the school welfare. That is money from the government. Now we are looked after by a married responsible adult. I am going to train to be a nurse one day."

Reeling with shock

"What a lovely girl," I said as Christabel ran back to join her team.

"Yes, isn't she? We are very proud of her. Now we will meet the rest of the ladies' teams."

I realized that our posse was minus one of its leaders. Fordson. I looked around. There he was, over on the field, bobbing and weaving in the thick of the football game, then thundering down the left-hand side with impressive speed. What is it about men and football?

Hmm, so we were to meet the team. I had never met a semi-professional football team before. They looked somewhat intimidating and I wondered if they would actually want to be met.

"Won't they mind us interrupting their game?"

"No, they are expecting you."

Expecting us? Why? As we drew closer I could see that they were completely absorbed in the matter at hand, the essential business of destroying their male opponents. I felt even more convinced that stopping to chat with visitors from England must be the last thing they wanted to do.

"Are we not going to be late for our meeting with the sex workers?" I asked, trying to decide in my mind which meeting scared me the most.

Patrick looked somewhat surprised.

"But these are the professional sex workers. The netball team and the women's football team. They are playing against the Corridor of Hope men's team. Got their work cut out, too. The men's team plays in the Zambian league."

Did he just say what I thought he said? A football team composed of sex workers? My brain reeled.

This is surreal!

A: A brief word from me about this same moment of discovery. Bridget says that her brain reeled. So did mine. It performed *Swan Lake* on a trampoline.

It has become fairly commonplace for people to attach the adjective 'surreal' to all kinds of situations and events.

"Climbing up into those mountains was surreal."

"The moment when I turned the exam paper over was truly surreal."

"You should have seen that electric storm last night. It was so surreal!"

"The instant when I knew I'd passed my driving test was just surreal."

Broadly speaking, people use the word to describe an experience that is striking or dramatic or odd or bizarre, and the *Oxford English Dictionary* does in fact now list the definition 'bizarre or strange' for this word. Hearing about these sports teams of female sex workers threw my mind back to the original use of the term, particularly in relation to the twentieth-century movement in art and literature, which aimed to express the subconscious mind through the juxtaposition of incongruous images. One thinks of melting clocks and levitating steam trains disappearing into fireplaces. I was also irresistibly reminded of a Monty Python episode back in the late sixties that included a football match between (as far as I can recall) the Brighton Gynaecologists, all dressed in gowns, caps and masks, and a team of parrot- and crutch-equipped Long John Silver imitators, none of whom was able to move from his position on the field because of having only one leg.

That was surreal, if you like, and so was this. For a moment or two I struggled to reconcile the concept of a well-organized, vigorous netball or football team with my stereotyped image of female commercial sex workers. A matter of vision, I suppose. Thank God that Patrick and his team at Chililabombwe have a much broader, more far-seeing vision than most of us.

Rapid readjustment

B: There were so many players, and they looked so normal, so dynamic and healthy. I don't want to give the wrong impression. Some of these girls did look pretty tough. But they had a warmth and closeness that was very endearing. Watching them giggling as they got into position for their photograph to be taken by Jim, I saw a natural openness and friendliness that was very attractive. It is easy in retrospect to imagine that all sorts of tragedies were etched into their young faces, but in fact they looked like a healthy, happy and motivated group of young women who were thoroughly enjoying themselves playing netball and football. That's the truth. Catching sight of several of the netball team members cuddling small children who were clearly their own, I realized that I was going to have to do some rapid mental readjustment and I am going to have to ask you to do the same.

In the case of Zambia and this situation in particular, you will need to remove from your imagination any images of sultry, satiny boudoirs and ageing, pouting seducers lounging on plumpy brocaded cushions, as well as more modern stereotypes. Substitute ordinary teenagers and young women who have reluctantly joined their trade through starvation and desperation. Some begin as young as twelve. Many are orphans. Some have babies. They clamber nightly into the cramped, sweaty sleeping compartments of stationary lorries to earn the equivalent, if they are lucky, of about £1 per client (double if they 'do it live' without a condom). They know the dangers. They may get beaten up or become pregnant. They may not get paid at all. They may contract AIDS and die in a few years. But where is the choice? If they do not eat, they and their babies will die in a few days.

That sports field seemed to us, in its own way, a triumph – a place of unconditional acceptance where, for a few hours every day, these girls are allowed to adopt an identity of which they can be proud. It offers them a chance to play, to recapture lost childhood. It is an island in the stormy sea of dangers that these girls regularly negotiate.

We loved being there, but suddenly it was time to move on yet again. It was time to visit the border between Zambia and the Congo, the place where most of the sex workers go looking for business.

The Kasumbalesa border crossing

An hour later, as I stood with Adrian in the fenced-off border area, I realized I would have to do even more mental gymnastics. This time it was my preconceived notions about the men who regularly engaged with sex workers that had to go. These men, because of the distance they travel through so many landlocked countries, are the most common carriers of the HIV/ AIDS virus, and are therefore largely responsible for the pandemic.

So now I ask you to remove images of overweight lecherous men on business trips with £100 notes bulging from Armani suits thrown carelessly over leather arm-chairs. Substitute ordinary workers, some barely out of their teens, stranded hundreds of miles away from their families. Congregating from many different cultures and speaking a variety of languages, these men and boys are forced to queue for up to three weeks, waiting for their papers to be processed in the petrol stinking dust of no man's land. Nose to nose the lorries stand, heaped high with goods bulging under greasy, rope-tied tarpaulins, destined very often for countries way beyond Zambia. The men dare not leave their trucks unattended because they would lose their precious jobs if there was any theft or vandalism. Or else they entrust their cargoes for short periods to lorry boys, many of whom are little more than children who got too hungry and ran away from home. Having hitched a lift, these boys are now thousands of miles away from home with little hope of ever returning. The loneliness and isolation created by this enforced idleness in a place which has no community, not even a common language, are almost tangible. Here at the Kasumbalesa border, perhaps the saddest, apparently most God-forsaken place we have ever seen, I begin to wonder. Is it so surprising that these men seek and pay for a moment of even simulated intimacy?

Yet it is here, because of the World Vision Corridors of Hope project, that the mustard seeds of a miracle have been planted ...

We had already witnessed this miracle of hope in the imaginative way in which near insurmountable problems were being tackled at the Drop-in Centre in Chililabombwe. Now, at the border, we had the chance to see it again.

Problem: how to communicate to the men the danger in which they are placing the girls, themselves and their families at home through declining to abstain from sex or use condoms. Solution: employ the services of unlikely heroes like the diminutive World Vision worker Doris – people who are prepared to go to the truckers and talk frankly to them. Even the sex workers love Doris and affectionately call out to 'Auntie Doris' as they dismount from the bus that brings them to work. Watching her in action as she drew herself up to her full five feet and good-humouredly challenged men who appeared to be twice her size about the dangers of their lifestyle was like watching Gideon in action against the Midianites. She is, of course, just one of the many peer educators whose tasks include distributing the government's supply of free condoms, offering practical advice and refuting some of the myths associated with sex and AIDS.

No, sex with a virgin does not cure AIDS.

No, it is not an insult to manhood to use a condom.

No, sex is not a taboo subject.

No, abstinence will not cause blindness (a convenient myth, this one!).

Yes, you should be tested to make sure you are free from HIV/AIDS and STIs.

Problem: How do we facilitate the testing? How do we draw in the frightened and the worried? How do we tackle the dangers of ignorance and taboos? We had already seen part of the solution at the Drop-in Centre in Chililabombwe, where men and women can receive counselling, avail themselves of HIV and STI testing, watch educational videos and enjoy coffee, friendship and a game of pool. Now we were seeing these questions addressed from another angle. A clinic right there on the border can put fears to rest and, if necessary, trained counsellors can help the men to realistically work through some of the questions regarding their uncertain futures before they move on. In one-to-one privacy men can be told exactly what AIDS is, how it spreads, how it can be prevented. They can ask questions. Even be shown how to use condoms. The time is right. Things are changing. Much of the defensive anger expressed in the past has gone. A lot of the men have seen their colleagues die. Deep in their hearts, many of them are very afraid.

And now, through consistent work by the Corridors of Hope workers in partnership with employers, some new patterns of thinking are emerging at every level. New dialogues are possible:

"Surely it would make sense for your drivers to be better informed of the dangers."

"We have wasted too much time. We have lost so many employees. Yes, to teach them is to make progress."

The Corridors of Hope staff are also tackling some of the sources of the problem. The actual length of time truckers are stuck at the borders is exacerbating the problem. Corridors of Hope workers are putting pressure on the bureaucratic departments responsible for the delays. Trying to persuade them to create a more efficient procedure. Making sure they have enough paper to be able to process the applications. Simple changes, many of them.

All of this is done with exceptional goodwill and lack of condemnation, summed up by the logo on one of the peer educator's colourful tee shirts. 'My friend with HIV is still my friend'. There is no blame. Only hope.

And they work so very hard.

The compound

"Of course, unless we get the Queen Mothers on our side our chances of success are very low."

I look at Adrian. Under normal conditions, the bizarre image of floaty pastel-coated ghosts wearing enormous tulle confections on their heads and bearing a marked resemblance to the Queen's late mother might be expected to evoke at least some response. As it is, the image flies past our imaginations to crash-land elsewhere – a testimony to the battering our brains and emotions have been subjected to throughout this long day. We are exhausted.

But the car we are travelling in has abruptly come to a halt, so it would appear that the day is not over yet.

"Wait for a moment. I will see if they are still here ..."

We watch Patrick's colleague run up a narrow path, unfasten a wire gate and disappear from view. What does he mean? Is who still here? Who have we still to meet?

"I'm sorry," Adrian returns to Patrick's remark. "Can you explain? Queen Mothers?"

"Oh, yes. Most of the sex workers we have around here live in compounds overseen by an older woman who looks after the girls. Organizes them. That sort of thing. They are women who have been involved in the trade but now are content to only do a little light work. The girls call them 'queen mums'. If they are supporting us they will make sure the girls are tested and let the peer educators come and see them. So you can see why it is important we set out to win their respect."

As we absorb this new piece of information and ponder what exactly light work involves, the gate swings open and Patrick's co-worker reappears.

"Yes. Yes. They are still here. Come, come."

We go.

Where, and to meet whom, we are not sure.

We enter a small courtyard surrounded by what look like chicken houses with wire meshing at the windows and small children pecking round the small dark doorways.

Rather more reluctantly, several young women also emerge, blinking, into the afternoon sunshine. Seeing that their visitors include familiar World Vision faces, their guarded expressions soften and toddlers are dispatched with urgent messages, presumably to summon the rest of the residents. Within minutes the yard has filled up with about twenty girls who sit themselves down in a group on the dirt floor. A few of them smile at us as they recognize us from the morning sports activities, and we finally realize that we are in the company of the border sex workers, many of whom we have already met. Stripped of the competent glamour lent to them by their football and netball strips they look puffier, pastier and much, much poorer. But the same closeness and interdependence are here. There is a lot of physical contact among them – arms lolling round necks, hands held, heads on each other's shoulders. It is as if they have literally become one in order to face representatives of 'the world', and there is an atmosphere of childlike vulnerability that we had not expected after our previous encounter.

Hanging on a sagging washing line suspended above the yard are the tiny scraps of fabric that I immediately recognize as 'tops'. Every parent of older teenage girls knows about tops. Overpriced miniscule fragments of poorly cut material, they breed in profusion in every household, a new one being absolutely essential to the success and feel-good factor of an evening out with friends. My daughter and her friends frequently exchange tops, their argument being that tops look totally different depending on who is wearing them. And, as the girls vary considerably in shape and size, that has to be so. I find myself wondering if these teenagers and young women do the same. I suspect they do, and a terrible sadness fills me as I think of them dressing up for the evening ahead, brushing their hair and applying their make-up. Telling each other they look nice. Envying each other's hair. Skin. Figures. Chattering as they clamber onto the bus. Having fun. So many things in common with girls the world over, except that in this case all the elaborate preparation leads only to the sad little corner of hell that we saw this afternoon.

The time has come for the inevitable. "What would you like to ask them?"

Nothing. Nothing. I want to take them away from this. I want it all to stop.

The downcast eyes of the huddled group in front of us reflect my tentativeness and fear. For the first time I sense shame, anxiety, discomfort. They don't want us to ask them anything either. Oh, well. Here goes.

"Umm, you seem very close … er … and important to each other. Is that … er … the case?"

There are several mumbled answers which Patrick enthusiastically interprets.

"Yes, yes that is true. They live as family. They say they share everything. They look out for each other."

"Look out for each other. Do you mean when you are at the crossing?"

Patrick doesn't bother to translate what he clearly sees as obvious.

"Yes, that is what they mean."

It would seem that the subject is now closed. In which case we are not getting very far!

"Er ... yes, but I was hoping they might tell us a little about what that means."

"Ah, yes, yes." Unperturbed, Patrick beams at the girls and explains.

One of the women, rather older than the rest, slightly raises her hand. Patrick smiles at her.

"Marjorie, you can tell us what we want to know." He turns his head to us. "She is the queen mum here. She knows."

Thank goodness for our short conversation in the car. Any last floating mauve figments drift away for ever. We've met Marjorie as a member of the football team. Thin, tough, with straggly long hair tucked under a tight-fitting red cap, I had assumed she was simply one of the girls, if a little older.

"Sometimes it is dangerous. You understand, sometimes when we go out one girl may come across a man and go with that man." We nod, trying to look as though that is the most natural thing in the world. "Then sometimes the man changes his mind. Maybe he beats the girl. But we have a system. If one of us gets a contract she tells a friend, shows her where they will be, which truck is his. So we know."

"And what if she shouted for help?"

There is such a voluble response to Adrian's question from almost all the girls that we get the strong impression there would be an extremely aggressive and instant response.

We are relieved to sense that the atmosphere in the yard is changing. The girls have expressed their solidarity and talked about something of which they can be proud. It seems a shame to change the mood, but we feel we must ask.

"What about protecting yourselves in other ways?"

Any attempts to be subtle are rolled flat by Patrick, who asks the girls, "Our visitors wish to know, do you insist on a condom being used?"

Their responses are bright and immediate.

"Oh yes."

"Life is precious."

"We insist."

"No condom, no sex."

"We say always use."

"We have seen friends get sick, so we know."

Patrick looks pleased, as of course he should. The message has clearly been received.

So why do I still feel so sad? Perhaps it is because this parrot-fashion acquiescence reminds me of girls I have looked after in care who know all too well the right and expected answer that will please, but who do not bring this information to bear on their practice.

If a girl is offered twice as much by a client to 'do it live', and if it is just her, alone in a cab, will she stick to her newly learnt principles? Especially if it might make her client angry, or if it means he doesn't pay at all or beats her? Do these women, like all of our teenagers bombarded with information about the dangers of smoking, believe bad things will never actually happen to them? Do they really care about themselves enough to bother? When the extra money means there will be enough left over, after the costs of staying alive, for the little extras that make life fun, like make-up and clothes? Did we always manage to do the sensible thing when we were young? Do we now?

But is it worth pursuing this line? Probably not.

We move on to asking them about their futures and learn that all of them would give it up if there were alternatives. They are absolutely unanimous in their vigorous head-nodding, causing Patrick to beam even more broadly. Again I feel doubts niggling. I remember Violet telling me about the deep psychological damage inflicted by having sex with a different man every night. I think of how isolated most of these girls have become from their communities and from their churches. How hard it would be to leave the compound where they are accepted for what they are, and go back. I remember the terrifying one-in-four Russian roulette statistic. I acknowledge the problems of finding alternative occupations that pay the same money, and suddenly I feel something close to despair. I sense a similar slump in Adrian, who is sitting beside me. And then something happens to jerk us out of our despondency.

The peer educators arrive, bursting round the corner of the compound in their brightly coloured tee shirts, scooping up excited children, settling into corners with groups of willing girls to look at and discuss the pictures of truckers and sex workers which form the basis of their educational materials. It is time for us to go, but no matter. Something real is going on, and it has lifted our spirits. A few of the girls look up and wave, but they are too absorbed with their friends for our departure to mean very much. They are with people who make them feel good about themselves. People who care and believe in their potential. I look across at Marjorie, deep in conversation with Veronica. I remember the life-affirming activities of the morning. The unconditional love and the unremitting hard work at the Drop-in Centre. The pool table. The new clinic. Chilufya. Auntie Doris. Christabel. I think of the Sanduka project, about which we have heard such amazing reports and which we will soon be seeing for ourselves.

The steps may still be tentative, perhaps even one forward and two back at the moment, but I am pretty sure that more and more of these girls will in time follow their leaders away from self-destruction and down the corridors of hope towards a new life. The dance, to a rhythm of life and hope, gathers momentum.

A story for Chilufya and all other prodigals

A: It was a warm summer evening, and the father of the prodigal had asked for a gathering to take place in the open space outside his home. The thronging crowd included all the members of his family, as well as close neighbours and good friends, not to mention every single man, woman and child who worked for him or lived beneath his protection. Such a comprehensive gathering had never been known before, and the reason for it was a mystery to all.

Standing at the doorway to his house, the prodigal's father, seeing that all were now present, bade the entire company sit. He waited for complete silence to fall, and then he spoke.

"I thank you for coming here today. I am anxious that all should hear what I have to say on this single occasion, so that I will not be obliged to repeat it many times."

He paused and sighed deeply, before continuing in softer, sadder tones.

"You will be aware – you cannot fail to be aware – that one of my sons, my youngest son, has been gone from my home for many months. He asked me to give him his share of the inheritance that would one day be his due. It was his desire to leave this place and seek a new life elsewhere. It was, as I am sure you understand, neither my will nor my wish that he should do this. The pain of parting with him was almost more than my heart could bear."

The old man held a paper up in his right hand for all to see.

"Here is a letter, brought to me by a member of my household this very day. It contains details of the life that my son is living now, the dark and terrible things that fill his hours in the far country to which he has travelled. The person who brought this to my attention spoke with bitterness and derision of my boy, clearly anticipating that I would welcome and indeed echo his condemning tone.

"My oldest son, in conversation after conversation at the family table, has mocked the very notion of his younger brother being of any value to me now. His words are harsh and unyielding. They are filled with hate. He seems to think that he pleases me with such cruelly dismissive speeches. Perhaps he assumes that I fail to voice agreement only because the scorn and fury in my own heart are too profound for words.

"Other, gentler souls have intimated their sympathy for me in losing a son to such disobedience and wickedness. They counsel me to forget that I ever had a younger son. Let it be, they advise, as though he never was your son. Let it be as though he were dead. Then you will find peace."

There was another moment of silence as he gazed at the faces in the crowd. When he began to speak once more it was with a passion that broke like thunder across the heads of his listeners.

"There is only one thing that will bring me peace! Only one thing that will heal my broken heart. And that will be the homecoming of my beloved youngest son. Yes, I wept when he departed. Yes, I begged him, for his own sake, to stay. Yes, I know all too well that the life he lives in that place is one of sin and degradation, a denial of all the right and good things that he once learned at my knee. But now, I wish all of you to hear these words. I love him.

I love that boy without condition. I yearn for him. I hold him in my heart, in my memory, in my mind, during every hour of every day. If you truly believe that this is not so, then you certainly do not know me. There has been no lessening of my love for him and it is a love that will never die.

"I will not force him to return home. He is where he wishes to be, and I must be here. I am what I am and he is what he is. I will live forever with the pain of loving him from afar if that is what the future holds. But let me tell you this. At the very instant when that dear lad of mine decides to leave his life of darkness behind and come back to the place where he belongs, I shall run to meet him, and I will enfold him in my arms, and I shall shower him with presents, and I shall throw a party the like of which has never been seen in this household or any other household before.

"You, all of you, do not dare to speak slightingly of the son that I adore. Do not disrespect the hope of my heart. Do not cause me more pain than I already bear. Family, friends, members of my household, please be with me in this. If you love me, then love him. If you wish the best for me, then wish the very best for him. If you speak of me with warmth and respect when I am not present, then speak in the same way of this son of mine who I hope will one day return to my embrace.

"And if," concluded the old man, his voice breaking a little, "you should happen to encounter him on your travels, do not fail to let him know that there is a father who watches for him every day and offers nothing but love and rejoicing if he should return. I thank you all for listening to me."

The crowd sat in silence for some minutes after the prodigal's father had turned and disappeared into his house. Then, one by one, they slipped quietly away.

10. Last Day in Zamtan

A: We went back to Lackson and Philemon's tumble-down house on our last day in Zamtan. They were the only community residents whom we specifically insisted on revisiting. Why was that? Who was this second visit for? For them? We thought so at the time. For the readers of this book? Perhaps. For us? Yes, in the end, I think it was for us, for Bridget and me.

There was something about those two boys; something about their enforced independence; something about the brotherly bond that, mercifully, enables each of them to know that there is at least one person in this world who really cares; something about the bravely lifted chin and defiant eyes with which carefully defended Lackson faces a world that challenges his ability to survive on every single day of his life; something about the small child in that same boy, a child who, we were convinced, remains alive and ready to be reached if anyone ever decides they would like to make the attempt; something about young, naturally charming Philemon, blessed with a gentle charisma that glows from the very centre of his personality; particularly perhaps, there was something about the consistently tough struggle that these brothers are bound to face if they really do want to rise from the dire circumstances they are in now, and eventually don those smart uniforms of theirs, potent symbols of a shining future life that, at present, exists only in their dreams.

Our three sons are all grown up now, and our family life was as variable in quality as anyone else's, but there was an ache inside Bridget and me when we compared the lot of these two teenaged brothers with the comforts and opportunities that our boys had known. It was painful. It was like a wound that weeps. It did not heal well. Especially not in the late evening, when we thought about them shivering through another African winter's night.

On the evening after our first visit to Lackson and Philemon we rang our middle son, Joe, who works with autistic children a few miles down the road from us in Brighton. We told him about the boys.

"What are you going to do for them?" was his immediate query. The idea that we might not do anything for them did not even occur to him.

"Well," replied Bridget, "I don't really know. We'd love to do something, but – I mean, we're supposed to do things that last – you know, things that are good for them in the long run . . ."

Joe snorted. He does a very good snort. On this occasion his snort, if we interpreted it correctly, was saying that if he was one of these two brothers, and he had a choice between being given real perishable presents now, or not being given anything at all because of some vague aid-agency philosophy to do with benefiting the community as a whole rather than gifting individuals, he knew which he would have preferred. And so, of course, did we. Funny how you don't know what you think until someone else tells you what they think and then suddenly you know that that's what you think as well – don't you think?

We checked with Fordson and Thom before actually buying anything for the boys, and they responded immediately and positively.

"Go ahead," they said, "good idea. We'll organize for them to be there."

Thus it was that, on our final day in Kitwe, we found ourselves strolling around the supermarket in the city, hunting for the aisle where the maize meal was kept. We were enjoying ourselves. Many people say that giving is much more fun than receiving as they grow older. I am sure the Bible is right in saying that it is more blessed to give than to receive, but a sort of mist forms around definitions of this statement when the most delightful gift you can receive is the gratitude of another person. We took pleasure in that brief shopping expedition for the two boys.

We had already bought two warm, woollen blankets in a shop further up the street. Now we just needed to dump two big bags of maize meal on our supermarket trolley and collect one other essential object that we were most likely to find up by the checkout counters.

Having found and collected the maize meal, we pushed our trolley along to the payment points, noting with interest and some surprise that in the place where sweets would normally be sold in a British supermarket, there were dispensing packs of MAXIMUM condoms at every checkout counter. Finally, at the end of one of the aisles, in a huge wire basket, we discovered a wide selection of the third item that we had decided (and Joe would certainly have agreed) was essential for the practical welfare of teenage boys. We bought them a real football.

Money to charity

Less than an hour later, the World Vision vehicle that had brought us to Zamtan via the supermarket dropped us, and the gifts we had bought, outside Rodrick's shop. We were a little puzzled as to why we had been dropped here instead of three-quarters of a mile away where the boys' house was located, but the mystery was solved when

Charity, her face wreathed in smiles, appeared carrying a pile of coloured lengths of material and hung them across the wooden railings at the front of the shop. Like it or not, I was about to keep that promise I had made at the Sports for Life day. Two or three other ladies immediately joined Charity, all with items for sale. Forgive me if I sound suspicious, but if ever there was a set-up, this was it.

We didn't mind. From a wide selection of tie-dye and batik work, we soon picked out four or five attractive examples of their wares. All that remained was to pay for them. Sound easy? Not for me. The following five minutes must qualify as one of the most embarrassing periods of my life. If you think I exaggerate, read on.

It was all to do with the blinking, blasted money. You see, there are no coins in Zambian currency – well, there may be, but we never saw any. All we saw was paper money, made up of innumerable separate denominations, each one printed in a different colour. Given that there are roughly 8,000 kwacha to £1, you can begin to appreciate what a thick wad of cash it is possible to accumulate in your back pocket in the course of a few days, even though the total value may not be more than £30. That was about the amount that I drew from my pocket when the time came to pay for our purchases. For once I found myself wishing that I had not dismissed the idea of using wallets some years ago for the good reason that I invariably lose them in the end. That money filled my large hand in a solidly congealed and untidy package. Approximately 250,000 kwacha had transmuted, through various transactions since our arrival, from large, manageable denominations into a plethora of every other possible value, including a rash of bright orange 50-kwacha notes, pretty to look at but worth, if my maths was correct, significantly less than one penny.

In a country so sorely afflicted with poverty it must have seemed to the onlookers who settled in a fascinated ring around me that I was positively awash with surplus wealth. To make matters worse – much worse – I was unable to see properly because I had forgotten to bring my reading glasses. Peeling all those notes apart and uncrinkling them and holding them up to the light to work out how much they were worth was like one of those dreadful fever dreams where you are doomed to do the same thing over and over again and you never get it quite right. A terrible business. After two or three minutes I felt like throwing all the money in the air and screaming. Nothing ever seemed to add up to the same total twice, whatever I did, while some of the notes, thin and faded from constant use, would have been difficult to read even if I had remembered my spectacles.

If only the assembled masses hadn't watched it all so intently. Not that they were upset or offended. On the contrary, my audience was blissfully happy. They clearly regarded me as a source of immense interest and entertainment. What fun to watch me fumbling clumsily through my cash, dropping the odd note every now and then so that I had to stop and pick it up and forget where I'd got to and have to start counting again. Eventually I resorted to the ploy of arranging little piles of equal-value notes in a row along the bench on both sides of me. It must have looked like the height of ostentation. It was also a calculated risk. One gust of wind would have taken me back to somewhere way before square one.

Needless to say, Bridget was not among those who were entertained by my multi-coloured, fluttering, dithering display. She made little sipping noises of exasperation throughout the proceedings.

It crossed my mind at one point that I might possibly have died and gone to hell. It really did begin to feel as if I was going to be there for ever, eternally damned to do ridiculously impossible division sums in my head and to squint at little coloured pieces of paper in the hope of making out what they were supposed to be worth. Finally, boggle-eyed and sweating, I was reasonably sure that I knew exactly how much money I had with me.

And, need I add, it wasn't enough.

Thankfully Peter stepped in with the shortfall, neatly extracted from a neat wallet in neatly arranged notes, and the nightmare was over.

Here's one I prepared earlier

We walked nearly a mile from Rodrick's shop to the place where the brothers lived, receiving puzzled stares from one or two of the locals as we did so. When we asked why this should be, Thom explained that it was rare for *musongi* (white people) to be seen walking anywhere in this community.

"Perhaps," I whispered to Bridget, "they think that we actually live in rows of four-by-four vehicles in England, a bit like hermit crabs in somebody else's shell . . ."

Our procession arrived at the house looking like a modern version of the colonial bush safari. Thom had insisted on carrying the blankets and the football in a bag, while the two sacks of maize meal balanced precariously on the handlebars of a bicycle. Somebody else toted the material that we had bought.

Philemon was there. Lackson was not.

As I have said, it is pleasant to give, and there was a little butterfly of excitement planing around in both of us as we presented Philemon with his gifts. We expected him to be a little overwhelmed by the arrival of a relatively large group of people bearing unexpected presents, but I think we were both taken aback by the way in which he took the bag from Thom without opening it or even sparing the contents more than a glance, and left it, next to the maize meal, beside a nearby tree.

We realized almost immediately that there were two reasons for this. One was that Lackson was not there.

"He wants his brother to come," explained Thom after a brief conversation with Philemon. "Someone has gone to find him and tell him to come."

My indulgent moment of disappointment passed. Of course he wanted his older brother there. They were a unit, a joint venture, two faces that became one when the world confronted them with problems or, more rarely, with pleasures. Now, something good was happening, and it was not possible for it to quite mean what it meant until Lackson was there to share it.

The other reason for Philemon's low-key response was a phenomenon that we have lost and, for all I know, never did have in our own society. Bridget encountered the same pattern of behaviour in Bangladesh at her first meeting with Shahnaj, our sponsor-child. Shahnaj took the wrapped presents that Bridget had brought from England and passed them, unopened, with no comment and the barest of acknowledgements, to her sister, who was standing beside her. Later, Bridget learned that it is considered very ill-mannered in Bangladeshi society to appear to value the gift more than the giver, especially if you have nothing to give in return, and I am sure that this was also the case with Philemon. The gifts could wait until we had gone.

A positive aspect of Lackson's delayed appearance was that Philemon became much more relaxed and talkative in his brother's absence, certainly more so than on our previous visit. Additionally, we had learned by now that the formal approach to interviews was a waste of time. It was far more useful to get down on the ground with the person you wanted to talk to, or at least to draw your chair close to theirs, rather than sitting at a distance in the middle of a row of visitors, as though some sort of job interview was being conducted.

We asked him how things were going with the rats. Shyly at first, but with growing confidence as he realized that we were genuinely interested, thirteen-year-old Philemon began to describe the hunting and cooking of bush rats in much greater detail than before. Suddenly animated, he sprung to his feet and disappeared into the little house, reappearing almost immediately with one of the wooden traps that we had been shown on our first visit. He laid it on the dusty ground before us.

"This is one of our traps for catching rats," he explained in his husky, hopeful voice, "it is made from wood and it has a metal spring on it that will jump back and catch the rats when they come to eat a groundnut."

A thought struck him. Once more he jumped up and disappeared into the house. This time, when he returned, he was holding a small, brownish nut in one hand, and a length of string in the other.

"I will show you. You see, here is a spike where we put the nut. I will show you what we do."

Anchoring the trap with his bare foot, Philemon threaded the string through the middle of the nut, impaled the nut on the spike, then tied the string to a simple lever that would release the restrained spring and send a bar attached to it crashing down on the unlucky rodent as soon as the cord was bitten through.

"I will show you just how it happens!"

Alight with the pleasure and pride of imparting specialized knowledge, Philemon raced into the dark interior once more, emerging again almost immediately with a box of matches.

"I will show you what happens when the rat bites the nut and breaks the string. I will use one of these to show you."

A match flared against the side of the box, and Philemon, reaching forward with the lit match in his hand and straining his face away from the trap as if an explosion was about to occur, directed the flame to the string, just at the point where it emerged from the nut. There was a moment of tension and then we all jumped as the string broke and the freed spring flew from one end of the trap to the other with a loud CRACK! causing the whole contraption to leap an inch and a half into the air.

"The rat is always dead," commented Philemon thoughtfully and superfluously.

We nodded our understanding. It was easy to believe that the rat would always be dead.

"Lackson is coming!" someone in the ever-present crowd suddenly called. "See over there! Here comes Lackson."

And indeed, when we sat up and twisted round in our chairs to look, there was Lackson, coming along the path that we had taken from the shop, walking at the speed of one who has been running but does not wish to seem to be in as great a hurry as he actually is. Soon he was beside his brother, guarded in his manner at first, taking in the visitors, the presents, the general situation, with a few brief glances around and a short conversation with his brother. In the course of this discussion Philemon must have passed on our deep and continuing interest in the whole rat issue, because Lackson, entering into the spirit of the thing, asked if we would like to see the remains of a cooked rat. Confident, presumably, that we were bound to say yes to such an interesting prospect, he disappeared into the house before we had a chance to answer, just as Philemon had done three times already.

"Here's one I prepared earlier," I whispered to Bridget and Peter as we waited. "Eat your heart out, Jamie Oliver!"

This foolish comment provoked a disproportionate amount of laughter, curtailed abruptly by Lackson's reappearance with a saucepan containing two disturbingly recognizable portions of cold cooked rat, one of them certainly a head, skin still attached. Infected apparently by Philemon's enthusiasm for imparting information, he told us that the preparation of this dish was very simple.

"First you cut the rat open," he explained, "and then you take out the intestines. Next you burn the hair off the skin in the fire, and then you can cook them in the saucepan. It is easy."

We nodded, busily taking notes like keen students on a home economics course.

Cut rat open.

Take out intestines.

Burn hair off skin.

Cook in saucepan.

Got it. Have a go for ourselves when we get home. Not.

In this more relaxed atmosphere I felt able to ask one of the questions that had been on our minds since that first meeting with the boys.

"When we saw you the last time you told us that you decided not to go with your grandma when she went back into the bush. You said that she was troubling you. What did you mean by that?"

"She was never satisfied with us," replied Lackson slowly.

His expression hardened at the memory, but there were audible vestiges of indignation and bewilderment in his voice as he continued.

"We were mistreated over food. When the time came to eat, the other children were given food and we were sent away to draw water or to cultivate. Those other children used to laze around while we worked and went hungry. We were mistreated. Also, we wanted to stay in a place where we can go to school. We would be in school today, but we are not because of the exams."

"And what are the biggest problems about living here?" asked Bridget.

There was a flash of eye contact between the two boys. I suspect that neither they nor we were in any doubt about what the answer to that question would be.

"Food," said Lackson, "that is our biggest problem. And clothing. And staying warm on these nights that are cold."

"What happens when someone gives one of you something – food, for instance? I mean, do you keep it all for yourself or do you give your brother some?"

No hesitation.

"We share everything we have. Sometimes we do have arguments with each other, but we share everything. Always."

It was time to leave. We shook hands with Lackson Banda and Philemon Lackson, then we stood with them for one awkward moment, failing to say all sorts of things that were washing around inside us. As we walked back up the track to meet the World Vision vehicle I looked back once. The brothers were standing outside their wreck of a house watching our departure, still not investigating those fine gifts that we had brought.

"Oh, well," I said to Bridget, "at least they'll eat tonight and for the next few nights, and those blankets should help to keep them warm, shouldn't they?"

Bridget looked at me, and after a moment I had to turn my face away. She was right. We had done nothing.

Since returning from England I have told one or two people about those presents we gave to Lackson and Philemon. One person said, "Isn't it more likely that they'll sell the blankets and the football than actually use them for themselves?"

"What if they do?" was my reply. "They were gifts. They belong to them now. They can do what they like with them. That doesn't trouble me."

And it doesn't. What troubles me far more is the strength of my ongoing, obedient commitment to needy children like those two brothers. As Shakespeare almost said, but didn't quite:

Who takes a gift from me takes trash,

'Twas mine, 'tis his,

But he who filches from me my treasure in heaven,

Well, that's a different pair of trousers altogether.

God bless you, boys. Looking forward to seeing you in those uniforms.

The last supper

B: It was with some relief that I returned to our guest house on that final afternoon to pack. It had been a good experience to see Lackson and Philemon again, but this particular *musongi* had a backache and was looking forward to a bath and supper.

Our last night in Kitwe was, we all agreed, only going to be truly memorable if spent in the company of the two men who had accompanied us throughout our stay and made it such a warm and special experience. Fordson Kafwetu and Thom Kasuba. We invited them to dinner, including in the invitation their wives, Prisca and Loveness, who I had been dying to meet and who I suspected might be fed up with all the extra hours their husbands had worked on our behalf. We knew that World Vision salaries rarely stretch to such treats as meals out. Both wives work full time, Prisca as a nurse and Loveness as a teacher. Prisca supplements their joint incomes by rearing broiler fowl to make ends meet. To our delight, their children were also going to be allowed to join us for this very special occasion. Fordson's three little girls were Light, aged two, Blessing, aged six, and Mercy of God, who at eight knew exactly what she was going to be when she grew up. She would be a bank manager. Then there were Thom's son, little Thom, and his daughter Chilisia, who loved reading and was planning to be an electrical engineer one day.

There was such excitement when they all arrived. Much jostling over who would sit with whom. A lot of laughter. Getting a meal for twelve people proved a bit of a challenge for the kitchen at the guest house where we were staying, but it gave us a valuable glimpse of just how much families have in common wherever they are living and whatever traditions they come from. The

smaller children, for example, began by being wildly
excited purely because they were up past their bedtime. It
was an excitement that turned slowly to bored fidgeting
as their food took what must have seemed an eternity to
arrive and they became cold and tired. When it finally
arrived there was a general revival as all the children
except little Thom tucked into – yes, you've guessed it,
burgers and chips with tomato ketchup! None of them
actually finished their meals, but all of them managed ice
cream! Little Thom, meanwhile, ate nothing, but drank
three bottles of Fanta which turned him into a giggling,
bouncing, firecracker. He only settled when he was
allowed to snuggle on his mummy's knee and eat half of
her pudding, the so-called 'cake of the day'.

Looking out at the swimming pool, tantalizingly
beautiful in the spotlights, its alluring turquoise stillness
belying the fact that it was in fact freezing cold, I felt
extraordinarily happy to be part of this. To be able to
listen to Loveness sharing her frustrations as a
schoolteacher about how often her pupils missed school,
sometimes for months at a time, because they were caring
for sick parents. To have the chance to sympathize with
Prisca's despair at the lack of drugs available in the
health centre where she worked. To be allowed to tune
into the exhaustion that is constantly a factor in both
Fordson's and Thom's lives, as pressures of work mean
that they often do not leave their office until after
midnight. To overhear Blessing whispering that she
couldn't remember if she had thanked Jesus for her
supper because we had said grace so long ago, and
watching her entwine her tiny fingers into her mummy's
hands as together they whispered another little prayer
just in case Jesus had forgotten the last one. To watch
Light, bouncing on her doting father's knee, singing
'Twinkle, twinkle little star' in immaculate, flute-clear

English. To play peekaboo with her through our fingers over the table. To witness the pride in Chilisia's eyes as she talked of her daddy's work. To feel Mercy's hand creep into mine as she sat next to me.

These are privileges which should really be shared by all those who, through regular giving, make the work possible, but I enjoyed them immensely and guiltlessly anyway.

There was only one jarring note in the whole evening. It was late. The air was becoming chilled. The only heat and light came from small wire braziers of burning coals set at intervals between the tables. When it had grown so dark that we could hardly see each other across the table we all agreed reluctantly that the time had come to say goodbye. Fordson gathered his flock and headed for his borrowed car. Thom went to phone for a taxi. It was at this moment that little Thom, who until now had persisted with his firecracker impression, noticed that his father's chair was empty. Suddenly fearful, he froze and spoke the only words he was to say all evening.

"Where's my daddy gone?"

His panic lasted only seconds. Thom returned almost immediately and scooped his small son up in comfortable, safe arms.

As we sat drinking coffee in the gloom after both families had left, we talked about that moment.

For little Thom, the anguish had lasted for less than one minute. For children all over Zamtan, Zambia and throughout sub-Saharan Africa, the bewilderment of separation never ends as they cry into the unanswering darkness:

"Where's my daddy gone? Where's my mummy gone?"

11. Sanduka

B: Leaving Zamtan was hard, but our sadness was tempered by the knowledge that we were going to visit a project that had become a legend in our minds over the last few days, especially during time spent at the Kasumbalesa border where the staff of Corridors of Hope had spoken to us of what they saw as their greatest challenge. How can the girls be persuaded to risk turning their backs on their jobs as commercial sex workers when, as a consequence, they may not be able to care for their babies and feed themselves? How can they turn their lives around and return to their communities with their heads held high? How can they be made safe?

They had told us of a solution already existing elsewhere in the country. A programme funded by churches and individuals in the UK which was taking girls off the streets and training them in commercially viable skills including tailoring, tie-dying, catering and hairdressing. Or returning them to school to complete their education so that they can go on to join a profession such as nursing or teaching. A programme in which spiritual and psychological counselling is offered alongside practical training. A programme that supports the girls by providing free lodgings and a small allowance to live on. A programme that enables them to sit government exams and gain accredited certificates from the institution, which are important in developing their sense of a new identity. A programme that, on graduation, presents each student with the essential equipment she will need to live independently. A hairdryer, perhaps, or a sewing machine. This programme is called Sanduka, which means 'deep change', and it has been running extremely successfully in Lusaka and Livingstone for the last two years. The sex workers invited to join this programme come from Chirundu, the border post between Zambia and Zimbabwe.

Of course, as their counsellor Eustacia explains, sitting with us in the car on our way to the Silesian Sisters centre in Lusaka where training programmes are operating, there are still bound to be hiccups.

Some are logistical. Living allowances are extremely small, making life while studying very challenging. Suitable accommodation must be found close to the training centres or schools so that the girls no longer need to live in the old compounds on the border and be tempted to supplement their incomes. Many are mothers, so there are small children who need to be looked after. Schools must be approached with tact. Then, after the girls qualify, where can they safely store their new equipment? How do they market their goods? How do they find suitable premises in which to establish a business?

The biggest problem, however, lies in the area of funding. Sanduka is an extremely expensive programme to facilitate. Even in Lusaka, where it has been proved an overwhelming success, there is money in place for only one more year. To set up an equivalent project near Chililabombwe is still only a dream. Consequently there is a huge waiting list, and at present only a few girls are being supported in this way. Finance even affects the spiritual and psychological aspects of Sanduka because money does not stretch to counselling rooms, and important confidences often have to be shared in leaky public corridors.

Despite all this, those working with these girls, Eustacia included, have been genuinely touched by the dramatic transformations they have witnessed. Of the 112 young women enrolled so far only four have dropped out – two of those, tragically, because they died of HIV/ AIDS. Everyone in the first cohort to take exams passed them. Already small businesses are starting up with several girls sharing premises for hairdressing or tailoring. Some of their textiles have been exhibited. One or two graduates are even involved in running workshops to help train others.

It was wonderful to hear so much good news. Settling back in the car, we allowed ourselves the luxury of window gazing at the sights of Lusaka. We passed hoardings advertising everything from shampoo to dog chains. We smiled at the 'Get Knotted' restaurant, marvelled at the number of churches, enthused about the flame trees, expressed our surprise over there being a Top Shop, and delighted in travelling along Cha Cha Road. Suddenly, Adrian let out a shout of laughter . . .

A matter of spelling

A: It was a sign near a roundabout that had made me laugh.

One or two letters out of place in a single word can make such a difference to the message imparted by a public sign. A couple of years ago I used a fictional context to describe an incident that really had happened to me. I was at Millmead Baptist Church in Guildford as part of a Bible Society tour. Before entering the building for the first time I happened to notice that a letter was missing from the three-dimensional sign on the front wall of the church. I supposed that it must have dropped off or been detached when something was thrown at it. Now, instead of being Baptists, members of Millmead appeared to have become part of some other bizarre sect entitled the BA TIST CHURCH. Never one to miss the chance of getting a cheap laugh, I began my talk by drawing attention to this, asking those present if they weren't just a bit tired of people taking the P out of the Baptist church. This pleasantry was greeted, as the great Richmal Crompton might have put it, with expressions of consternation from the expensive seats at the front, and ribald laughter from the cheap seats at the back. Since then I have taken a particular interest in public notices, and especially those on the outside of churches.

Perhaps that is why this particular sign on the edge of a large roundabout in Lusaka so readily caught my attention. You may be interested to hear, by the way, that roundabouts in Zambian cities are rather splendid at the moment. Quite a lot of scarce public money has been spent on plants, statues and monuments in order to instil a sense of dignity and well-being in those citizens who swirl around them on their daily grind from home to work and back again. A good idea, we thought. This sign was on a large banner supported by a pole at each end, and its aim was clearly to draw the attention of roundabout users to one of the local churches.

There are quite a lot of Christians all around the world who might have felt very drawn to this church as it appeared to be advertised. We live in an age where it is commonplace to hack and chip away at the Christian faith until it acquires a shape that will give in and comfortably admit whoever comes along. The cost of following Jesus is rarely preached, and it is possible to rationalize just about any sin of commission or omission as long as you approach it from varieties of obscurely creative perspective that find no home in the teachings of the master. Some of the so-called Christian responses to HIV/AIDS are good examples. Condemnation. Neglect. Sniffy, muttering disapproval. Self-righteous distancing from the problem. Downright meanness. Well, the good news for those who wish to maintain these attitudes is that there appears to be a church in Lusaka that is specifically designed to justify anything and everything that they choose to do or feel or say. It stands beside a roundabout that offers many possible exits, and it calls itself:

The Church of St Michael and All Angles

On the other hand, it may be just a spelling mistake . . .

Sausage rolls and stories

B: We were a bit late arriving at the Silesian centre, but Sister Joanna was delighted to see us. I suspect she had had a little difficulty persuading her students that it was worth staying past their normal finishing time to meet us. The atmosphere was slightly strained to begin with, but soon we all relaxed and the afternoon we spent with some of these brave young women, munching their freshly baked sausage rolls and admiring the cloth they had dyed, was one of the most inspiring of our trip – especially when we persuaded some of them to share their stories. Some were happy to speak in front of the others. One or two sidled shyly up to us afterwards to talk about the things that had happened to them.

I will not even try to describe the wariness, hesitation, anxiety, shame and tears that accompanied their words. Or the shining excitement in their eyes as they shared their hopes for the future, some of them for the first time. I will simply let them speak for themselves.

My name is Rita Muyunda.

I became a sex worker when I was twelve. I am now twenty-three. What happened to me was this. My parents died and I was an orphan. There was no one to pay for me to stay at school. No one to support me. So I went to stay with friends. Each night they got dressed up and went to the border crossing at Chirundu. To the trucks. I started to go too. At first it was not nice but I found I could have money to live. Then I met people from World vision who told me to stop doing this work.

I said, "How can I stop? I can only stop if you find me something else to do."

So then I started going to meetings at the Blue House. Every Friday I went. They were very friendly to me. I saw how these diseases came about. I learnt what the risks were. I decided I did not want to take these risks any more. You see I have a child, a little boy called Muyunda. He is two and a half years old. I do not want to make him an orphan. They said to me they cannot decide for me. I must decide for myself if I want to change my life. So I say yes, I would like to join Sanduka. I am told I can choose between tailoring and catering. So I choose catering and I have been here now for one year.

My name is Maureen Lungowe Muilela.

I am twenty-three years old. I have two children, a boy who is two years old and a girl who is five. My parents both died in 1999 when I was eighteen. I did not know I can be the person I am today. I joined the skills training course last year. We encourage our friends to leave sex working and join Sanduka. Some listen to us. Some don't, because they say there will still be financial problems. They think there will be nowhere to live but accommodation is found for us so we do not have to go back. If I have to go back to sex work I will get HIV / AIDS and die. This is my only chance.

My name is Judith.

My parents both died when I was quite young. I found life to be very difficult. So then I met a truck driver and he asked me to come with him to Chirundu. I came and I ended up being in the sex trade. I stayed in the community house and then every evening I would go with the other girls to the truck drivers. With the money I would buy food and also drugs. This makes me very ashamed. Then I had a child, Kafue. That was a good thing for me but my life was not good. Then one day the peer educators came and told me about HIV / AIDS. I did not know about these things before. So from then I began to go to the Blue House for counselling. There I was told that for those who really wanted to change there was a project offering skills training. Or indeed you could go back to school. You had to be picked because we were told this project cost a lot of money and only those girls who would really decide to change their lives should be the ones to benefit. Some only wanted the things they gave you. They had heard that at the end of the course you are given equipment for the job you have trained for. A hairdryer and other useful equipment if you are to be a hairdresser. Pots and pans, knives and utensils if you have done catering. A sewing machine and threads if you have taken the tailoring course. They wanted the things, you understand, but did not want to change. But I did want to change so much. Because I wanted a new life for me and for Kafue. And now I feel different about myself. I am busy. There is no need for me to start doing anything bad. I feel at home. I have hope.

My name is Laura Ngosa.

I have a daughter. She is eleven years old and she lives with my mother in the Copperbelt. I can go and see her in the holidays but I am only allowed to visit her in my mother's house. My mother does not allow her to travel to stay with me in Lusaka. Maybe she does not yet trust me to be a good mother. But one day. When I have finished my training and have my certificate maybe I will have proved myself worthy.

My name is Cecilia Nalungwe.

I have a child, a little girl. She is three years old. She lives with my cousin during the term time because I am so very busy. Then I see her in the holidays. I am doing the catering course here. I came from a border town in Tanzania in a truck. I decided to travel because my friend had told me about her job as a sex worker. It sounded the answer for me. I would have money. But it was not good. Many times I was not given money at all by the truck drivers. Then I met with the workers at the Corridors of Hope. They told me about the bad effects of my way of living and they told me about Sanduka. It was a new project. People in another country were to pay for some of us to leave our jobs as sex workers and start again to train for a new life. So I said I would like this very much. Because I thought to myself, "What if I stop? What if I go to school? Then I will one day surely have something better. My daughter will be able to live with me." I was chosen at the beginning. During the holidays I go to see my friends in the compound and tell them about Sanduka. I tell them to come to the meetings at the Blue House so they too can learn. And I tell them that one day I will own my own restaurant and that I will employ my friends!

My name is Catherine Mudenda.

I do still have parents alive but I come from a very, very poor family. I heard that at Chirundu you could earn money so I decided to come there and be involved with the sex trade. When I arrived I knew no one. Then I began to go to the truck drivers. Many, many drivers. So I decided this life is easy. I have money. After that I did not like it. I was cut off from my family. I drank a lot of beer to make it easier. I was not happy. Then I met people who came to the border to talk to us. We heard about the Blue House where we could go for counselling. I went and I learnt about how bad and dangerous my way of life was for me. So I asked to join Sanduka. Now I am even able to go home and see my family in the holidays. Sometimes it is hard work but I think to myself, "If I stop, what then?"

My name is Precious.

I was fifteen when I began work as a sex worker. I stopped when I was seventeen because I had a chance to join this project. I did well at school and now I am able to continue to learn. I have many friends here.

My name is Axilia.

I left my home to come to Chirundu and my family no longer wanted to know me because I was now a bad girl. I was very sad. Then I met the World Vision workers who encouraged me to come to their meetings every Friday. When I was told about Sanduka I was very encouraged. I was told I could choose between formal education and skills training. So I chose tailoring. But I had to wait then and see if I would be chosen. I least expected to be given a place. I did not even tell my family I had tried to get onto such a course. But when, at one Friday meeting, they told me I had been chosen I was so very happy. I went to my parents and I asked for their forgiveness. There were many tears together but my parents were so very happy. They forgave me. They really appreciated what the people who give us the money for our training are doing for all of us. Now I feel good. I am part of my family again and at last I feel good.

My name is Berry Mezimezi.

I have a little girl called Theresa. She is the most important thing in my life. She is staying with my cousin here in Lusaka. Every day I think of her when I am doing my catering training. I am so happy because now that I am no longer a sex worker, every evening I am able to be with her. To give her a bath. To sing to her. One day I will be able to look after her.

My name is Eunice Namiyobo.

I come from Nwamba and I have two children. My parents died in 1995. By then I had one child. Then two years later I had my next child. But their father was not good to us. He left us. I had a big problem. How would I manage to look after them? Give them food? Send them to school? Provide for them? So after thinking and thinking I knew I wanted one man so I could marry and then my children could go to school. But there was no Mr Right anywhere. Then one day I went to Chirundu. I left my children with their aunt so they can go to school and I sent money to my sister. I felt bad all the time but it was the only way I could see to help them. I missed them very much. Then one day I met some peer educators who had come to the border to meet us and to talk also to the truck drivers. They asked me if I knew what I was doing really. Did I understand the dangers? I was afraid. They advised me to stop and told me to come to their meetings. So I came every Friday and I was picked to come on a catering course. My children are well and happy. They are still with their aunt at the moment, but one day, when I have my certificate and my new job, they will be with me. I know this in my heart.

A: How God must rejoice over each one of these girls who is rescued from a life that must inevitably lead to, at best, nothing, and at worst, a miserable death. And what a celebration there will be for those who return to him. What gifts! A ring, a cloak, a feast and, most important of all, a safe place in their Father's house for ever and ever. They might even put on the occasional dance.

Epilogue:
Zamtan in Hailsham

A: "I wish I was God."

"You can be if you want."

I was walking the dog along a path near our home for the first time since returning from Zambia when this little snatch of inner dialogue occurred. For a moment I simply could not understand what the latter, six-word sentence that had entered my mind could possibly mean. As a reply to the ridiculous wish that I had expressed silently to myself it didn't seem to make any sense at all.

Could have been utter nonsense, of course. I am very wary about the whole business of God speaking directly to men and women, but I am also sure that we should remain open in our minds and spirits. After all, if for fear of sounding silly or being mistaken, no one speaks out about what God seems to be saying, how are we ever to benefit from the real thing when it comes? We certainly do not want to miss anything that we are supposed to hear. And why should we not have prophets in this age as much as in any other? Elijah in Epsom. Jonah in Jerusalem. Nathan in North America. Zechariah in Zambia. The Lord knows that we need them. Please speak to us, Lord. We will be wisely wary but we will also try to be willing. That seems to be the way.

There is a means by which I have learned to sense just a hint of the direction that might be right for me. It happens in the form of an inner conversation, usually initiated by my asking a question or making a comment. I take note of anything resembling a reply that forms itself in my mind, and perhaps continue with a further question, hoping that the other end of the dialogue will see fit to continue the exchange until some sort of useful conclusion is reached. These little personal dramas can be quite lengthy, or they can be very brief indeed. Now, you may be inclined to suggest that I am deluding myself if I seriously claim that the 'other end of the dialogue' is God. I don't blame you. I might even feel inclined to agree with you. In one sense, though, it doesn't really matter. If we are in a praying relationship with God, and we sincerely want to follow Jesus, and are ready to be wrong, and don't take ourselves too seriously, then we can explore these mental highways and byways and enjoy finding out where they lead.

"I wish I was God."

I had said those rather unthinking words because, having returned to England, I was suddenly aware of all the needy people we know in our own part of the world whose fortunes might change radically if God were to do some dramatic miracle in their lives.

"You can be if you want."

So, what could the second line of that little piece of dialogue possibly mean? I asked God to help me understand. Let me tell you what I decided those words might mean.

In Zamtan there were no Exodus-type miracles going on. No flocks of quail dropping from the sky, or manna raining down from heaven. Most people were hungry for much of the time. As far as we could see there were no dramatic healings happening in this community either. The people who suffered from AIDS, for instance, continued to suffer from the dread disease. They will suffer even more, and die sooner, without the provision of expensive, complex drugs. It was the same when we visited the slums of Dhaka in Bangladesh. The love of God was only being expressed in those endless acres of desolation to the extent that people were willing to practically serve those who were in need.

Do not misunderstand me. I believe in miracles. I really do. And I know that they can happen anywhere and at any time. But when you stand in these places, when you walk up and down the dusty trails of poverty-stricken, disease-ridden communities, you know – you just know – that the first call of God on those who claim to care is the same call that was received by Mother Theresa. It is the call to be his hands and feet. God with skin on, as someone once put it. Whether it is by going or by giving or by getting practically involved in some other way, we can be part of the sacrificial, generous love of the risen Jesus reaching out to a fallen, hurting world through his body on earth. And that is the greatest miracle of all.

Here in the West, here in our home town of Hailsham, there is plenty of food and water, excellent health care, housing for all and free education for every child.

But, God seemed to be saying to me, when I look at Hailsham, when I walk the streets of your town, I see Zamtan. I see a dusty wilderness. I see people who are impoverished and sick in their spirits. I see enormous need and very few people who are willing or brave or obedient enough to do anything about it. Who will be my hands and feet here? Which of you will stop playing religious games, a readily available luxury when your stomach is full and your house is warm, and take yourselves into this community so that, through you, they will meet me?

"But what is the scarce commodity that they need, Lord?" I asked. "In Zamtan everyone talks about 'food security', the safety of knowing that there will be something to eat today and tomorrow. What is the equivalent here? What is the one thing that these people are most in need of? Tell me what we should give them."

The answer to that question took some weeks to come. One evening Bridget and I visited the house of the local curate, Blair Carlson and his wife Elizabeth, for a meeting. His two blonde, beautiful little daughters were there as well. Megan is ten and Ellie is five. Clear-eyed and confident, this charming pair unconsciously worked the kind of magic on me that I have learned to expect from children who are truly loved and cared for. Daddy and mummy are good, kind people, therefore, they guilelessly reason, all other grown-ups must surely be just as good and kind. In a sense they placed the mantle of their parents on to me, as they probably do with all visiting adults. There is nothing more flattering or inspiring. Just for a little while, all you really want in the world is to come up to their expectations.

And that is the answer. That is the scarce commodity. We cannot be God, but we can represent him. We are called to put the mantle of our heavenly Father onto all those we meet, so that, like little children, we offer them the same love, respect and service that we offer to our God. That is what Mother Theresa meant when she said that she saw Christ in the faces of filthy beggars rescued from the streets of Calcutta, and that is what God asks us to see in the face of every single person we meet. It will be very far from easy. It will require an act of the will and a great deal of effort and a lot of prayer, but we are the minority in possession of this scarce commodity, so we had better get on with it. It is faith in practice.

Out of all this comes a fearful truth about evangelism that is central and inescapable in Zamtan, Dhaka, Hailsham or anywhere else you care to name. If people are not able to meet Jesus in us, there will be little point in talking about him.

We pray for God's rich blessing on every one of us as we work out how and where best to serve him and those he loves. If you and I are not already helping, now might be the time to begin. If you already give, why not give more? The Son of God is dancing to the rhythm of his Father's love. We are warmly invited to join hands with our partners in the dance.

Making a Difference

Reading a book like this provokes one guaranteed reaction – 'what can I possibly do to make a difference in places like Zamtan?'. The answer is that, for what may seem like a very little time or money, you can do a great deal.

Make a donation: By making a gift you can help World Vision to bring support to communities like Zamtan where HIV/AIDS is having such a devastating impact. Send your cheque payable to 'World Vision' to HIV/AIDS Appeal, World Vision, Opal Drive, Milton Keynes MK15 0ZR, United Kingdom.

Child Sponsorship: For the price of not much more than a daily cup of coffee you could sponsor a child in a World Vision long-term programme in Zambia or neighbouring countries where HIV/AIDS is making a major impact. Your financial help will take the community forward, and your link with a child will enrich their life and yours too.

Alternative Gift Catalogue: For an inspiring alternative to predictable presents, our Gift Catalogue lets you 'give' friends and relatives things like chickens and pigs that actually go to some of the world's poorest people. The catalogue includes gifts relating directly to World Vision's response to HIV/AIDS.

Use your will: The battle against HIV/AIDS is going to be here for a long time yet. Including a designated gift in your will is a way to bring hope and help to a generation to come.

Make your voice heard: Contact your MP and your MEP and ask him or her to encourage the UK government to champion the cause of HIV/AIDS – in particular the needs of orphans and vulnerable children. Visit the World Vision website (www.worldvision.org.uk) for details of World Vision's campaign on this issue.

For details on all of the above just call our help team on +44 (0)1908 841010. Or visit www.worldvision.org.uk

World Vision